THIS IS A PRACTICAL MARKETING BOOK,

that has grown out of the ideas that were developed and tested in a series of live workshops at coworking and "learning-by-doing" spaces the 3rd Ward and General Assembly.

That means we are about to start a massive brainstorming session. Get out your laptop, pen, paper, or whatever you like to work with and let's start exploring your marketing possibilities. We want you to write in the book, to make it your own.

Your goal is to find two or three practical tools and ideas you can implement right away, even tomorrow. We've kept theory to an absolute minimum. Don't stress about trying to "get" everything or applying every idea to your business. Take what works for you and focus on that.

That's the book. Now, who are you? Do you create art? Do you run a small business? Do you sell a product, offer a service, or run a store? This book will help you navigate the online world of Facebook, email and SEO to reach more people and sell more product. We'll show you how to do that in an honest and creative way.

It probably feels a little overwhelming to figure out where to start. And if you're already using the Internet to market your business, you want to know if you're doing it right and if there is more you could be doing. AND DO I NEED A TWITTER ACCOUNT OR WHAT?!

WHAT ARE MY GOALS?

Here are some things you might be trying to do in your business:

- Grow your customer list.
- Connect with people in your area who need your service.
- Keep your best customers coming back.
- Create a community for your customers.
- Let your customers know about daily specials and important news.
- Have your customers tell their friends about your product.

Start by creating a list of the goals you have for your business — RIGHT NOW! This list will include the things you want to do to grow or support your current business.

1. _____

2. _____

3. _____

You will return to this list throughout the book. If one of the tools you learn about helps further one of your goals, prioritize that tool. If not, return to it later.

WORKSHEET

In order to get the most out of this book you need to fill out the worksheets at the end of each chapter. Each chapter will get you brainstorming and inspire you to come up with new, interesting and fun ways to use digital marketing. By the end of the book you'll have many new ideas you can start using right away. The ideas you come up with by filling out the worksheets will help you to navigate the seemingly difficult and sometimes frustrating world of digital marketing.

There is no *right* way to start digital marketing and no set order on what to do first. This is why it seems daunting to some and thrilling to others. We recommend going with your favorite idea. Maybe it's having a great email list or maybe it's improving customer loyalty. Whatever it is, pick one thing and go after it. Let's get started!

PS

If you bought this book in electronic format, you can download the worksheets here « ericmorrow.com/worksheet » or send an email to « digitalmarketing@ericmorrow.com » stating where you purchased your copy of the book and we'll send you a PDF version that can be printed.

WORKSHEET

TABLE OF CONTENTS
DIGITAL MARKETING FOR EVERYONE

CHAPTER 01
YOUR DEMOGRAPHIC

This book was written with you, THE CREATIVE ENTREPRENEUR, in mind. For our purposes, a creative entrepreneur is anyone who is making something new that he or she wants to sell or promote; you may be an artist, an independent business owner, a personal trainer, a mid-sized software company, a musician—anybody! The unifying characteristic is that the creative entrepreneur takes initiative and accepts the risk of failure—and the rewards of success!

TAKEAWAYS

- Who is most likely to buy something?
- Don't be generic. Be very specific. Your demographic doesn't include everyone.
- What is your story? Why are you doing what you do?

The best way to market your business is to get to know your customer. Once you know your customer, you can give them the absolute highest value product or service. Your customer base is called your demographic. You want to know everything there is to know about your demographic.

Demographics contain a few key characteristics, such as:

- Age
- Sex
- Location
- Income
- Favorite magazines, websites and hobbies
- Marital status/Kids

The biggest marketing mistake you can make is to say "I'll sell to everyone." Most likely your product or service won't appeal to everyone and you'll miss your niche by trying to market to everyone. Instead, a more profitable move is to find the niche demographic interested in your product and aim your marketing directly at them.

Next, you will see a sample chart we created to help you define your target demographic.

STEREOTYPICAL TARGET DEMOGRAPHICS FOR NYC

Stereotype	Location	Income	Age	Sex	Favorite Magazine
Soccer Mom	UWS	$100K	35	F	Lucky
Corporate Executive	Financial	$250K	50	M	Economist
Hispter	Brooklyn	$50K	23	M	Something you've never heard of
Student	NYU	$10K	19	F	Wired
Retiree	Queens	$30K	65	F	Golf Magazine
Sports Fan	Bronx	$40K	27	M	Sports Illustrated

The chart above is grossly stereotypical (we put the name right there at the top!) But it should help you start thinking about who your demographic is. Go ahead and circle the cell in each column that you think most accurately describes your demographic. For example, Elissa is a personal trainer who owns MomUp! Her demographic is the soccer mom or sports fan, living in lower Manhattan or Brooklyn, with an income of $85k and up, with an age range from the low-30s to mid-50s, both men and women, who probably read Sports Illustrated or Lucky (fashion and fitness frequently go hand in hand).

Once you have a sense of your demographic, you can move on to the rest of this book. We will talk about what type of content you should create and many ways of attracting attention to your product or service. But you must know who your demographic is. The first way to figure that out is to look at your sales. Identify who your best customers are and who your most frequent customers are. Take those customers and look at the chart above to define them. If you're still not sure, try asking your friends, customers, and people who are familiar with your business.

If your business is brand new, think about your potential customers. Who will most likely be your first customer? What are they interested in and what problem(s) will your business help them solve? Don't stress about getting this exactly right—as your business moves forward you will continually define your exact demographic.

BOTTOM LINE

You need to know what type of person is most likely to buy your product. You want to direct your marketing to the specific group of people who are already more inclined to purchase your product. Know who your ideal customer is.

DEMOGRAPHIC EXAMPLES

If you're still wondering who your demographic is, take a look at the demographics of some of the people and companies with whom we've worked. (Note: some names and companies have been changed at the request of the owners). Throughout the book we are going to introduce many different businesses to you and give examples as they relate to each chapter.

BED AND BREAKFAST : Mark and Eleanor are inn owners in Bar Harbor, ME. Their target demographic is both men and women (normally couples), age 45 and up, predominantly located on the east coast of the United States, making $100k+, interested in being very comfortable near the outdoors (their inn is located at Acadia National Park), and want the coziness of staying at a small, family-run hotel.

MUSIC : Laurie Berkner is a children's recording artist. Her target demographic is 25-45 year old mothers living in the United States. Most make at least $50k a year, are college educated and read mom- or family-related websites and publications.

EDUCATION : Rick is a tutor. He works with high school students, predominantly on the SAT and math. His students are mostly 14-18 years old (in high school), although some continue with Rick after going to college. He works with students in New York City, mostly on the upper east and upper west side. His students are technically his customers, although their parents pay for the service. Both his customers and their parents are well educated, placing a priority on getting into high-ranking universities.

HOME : Metro Screenworks specializes in anything that separates your house from the outside world. Their target demographic is anyone who needs a new screen—usually a screened door or window. These people are more likely to be middle class with homes they carefully maintain in good neighborhoods.

EXERCISE : Elissa is a personal trainer. Her company is called MomUp! She teaches group classes for new moms in gyms around the city. She's met many of her customers through her classes as they try to shed their pregnancy weight. Her demographic is women, with total household earnings over $85K, busy schedules, who are body conscious and interested in educating themselves on better ways to stay healthy after having a child.

SOFTWARE : ColSpace makes media planning software. Their clients are predominantly major international brands with large advertising budgets, and the media agencies that serve them.

FISHING : Sara's family runs a fishing supply business in rural Pennsylvania. Their clients are local sporting fisherman. These clients are mostly male, making around $30K a year and who might enjoy a new piece of fishing equipment for a gift. They are mostly hobby fishermen.

DANCING : Tiffany and Rodg run a dance studio in Westchester, NY. Their main customer base is single men and women 24+ who make above $40K a year and want to learn to dance. Their secondary customer base is couples preparing for their upcoming weddings.

TOM'S RECORD LABEL

Tom Goss is a musician. He sells music (CDs and downloads), t-shirts and concert tickets. He lives in Washington, DC with his husband Mike.

TARGET DEMOGRAPHIC

Tom's audience is defined primarily by sexual identity. The audience is predominantly gay men whose age range varies widely but leans towards the 30s and 40s. Their geography is spread out across the entire country (and he even has some non-US fans). Because music is so easily purchased and consumed over the internet, this is quite feasible. Income is also quite varied and not too important to Tom. The price point on his CDs and concert tickets is affordable ($20-30). His most avid fans make active use of Facebook—where Tom connects with them on a daily basis. His fans tend to listen to other gay musicians, are strongly in favor of gay marriage, and listen to gay radio stations and TV channels (like MTV's Logo).

JANE'S PET SHOP

Jane Simpson is the owner of a small, boutique pet shop in downtown Manhattan that specializes in high-end dog clothes, leashes, beds, toys, dog food, grooming tools and all sorts of other canine products.

TARGET DEMOGRAPHIC

Jane's target demographic is the successful professional who is also an avid dog lover. They are usually between 25 and 40 years old. Most of her clients don't have children and see their pet as the center of their lives. They want to have the very best for their pet. Her clients make over $150k a year and tend to work long hours. They prefer to pay more for high quality supplies.

CHAPTER 02
WEBSITE CONTENT

ColSpace had a website that was ten years old. It even said so, down at the bottom of the page: "Designed in 2002." The company's product had changed quite dramatically in the intervening decade but the website hadn't kept up. When potential clients would visit the site, it wasn't immediately apparent what ColSpace was selling or even what ColSpace really did! In short, the website wasn't helping ColSpace win any new customers.

ColSpace sells a media management application that allows big companies to keep track of where they are spending their advertising dollars across different media types, such as TV and radio. Matt Greenhouse, CEO of ColSpace, decided to update the site. Websites commonly have four types of content: text, pictures, video and audio. We built content around these areas. For text we had simple descriptions of the product, the company, and how another company could start working with ColSpace. For pictures we created a product tour that highlighted different aspects of the software. For video we got a little more creative and created animated shorts that tell ColSpace's story and describe its product in an entertaining and succinct fashion.

- Your website is your company's home base.

- It should provide educational, interesting or helpful content for your customers.

- The four most common types of content are text, pictures, video and audio.

CONTENT FOR YOUR WEBSITE

Maybe you're about to start building your website or maybe you've got one that's up and running. Either way, the first thing you want to think about is who is going to your site and what information you need to provide for them. Your home page should explain at one glance what your business is about and whom it will serve. You don't get a second chance to make a first impression, so don't take your homepage design lightly. Look at other websites of similar businesses and see what they do right and what they do wrong. Is it easy for you to understand what they do? Is it easy to see how to navigate to the next step or page?

The rest of your website should support the needs of your customers. Let's look at the homepage for the website of a restaurant. Ask yourself what it is that people who come there want to see and do. The name of the restaurant should be listed. Visitors should know, without more than a second's look at the page, how to view the menu, the restaurant's location, reservation number, pictures of the food and the interior of the restaurant.

These are the nuts and bolts of content. Provide the information that your customers want. Are you offering a new online service? Explain right away what that service is. Are you a photographer? Include various galleries of your work so customers can flip through and get an immediate idea for the feel of your work.

Content is the heart and soul of your marketing and should get the attention it deserves. Marketing is mostly about educating your customers about what you do; your website content is how many of your customers will learn about your product or service. The goal of the content on your site is to make it perfectly clear to the customer what they are getting, what problem it will be solving, how much it costs and what their life will be like after they buy your product.

Next, you'll want to consider how to convey content to your customers. Again, you need to know your demographic and what they are there to see or to learn. Each of these four types of content can be used to get information to your customer. You need to think about the best way to support your site. Should a restaurant have an audio file that lists their menu? For most people, that isn't the easiest way of learning what dishes the restaurant is offering.

TYPES OF CONTENT

TEXT (WRITING) is where most people start. This can take the form of product webpages, descriptions of your service, or a blog. For the true business parts of your site it is important to make your text as clean, simple and descriptive as possible. There shouldn't be any confusion about what you're selling! This isn't to say you can't have any personality, particularly depending on the industry you're in. Many Business-to-Customer (B2C) sites have lots of personality - like Zappos or MailChimp. Compare MailChimp to ConstantContact though and you'll see the difference between a site (and presumably a company) with a quirky personality and one that is "corporate". The best thing to do is have the text of the site reflect your personality and the personality of the company. Remember that you aren't trying to please everyone. You only need to please and attract your target customer.

PICTURES are a great way to introduce people to your company because pictures are easy to flip through. You can have pictures of just about anything - your product, your results (if you deliver a service), events you've hosted or attended, and satisfied customers (with testimonials!). Pictures are also a great way to explain what you do when accompanied by text.

VIDEO is one of the most effective ways to engage your customers. Especially when a new customer first finds your site; a 30-second intro video can quickly explain what you do, what your value proposition is, and what life will be like for your customer after they purchase your product or service. And making this type of video is a great way of figuring all of these things out! Check out sites like ColSpace.com, Hiplok.com and Dropbox.com for examples of effective intro videos (as of the writing of this book in October 2012). You can also make video explanations of your product (see metroscreenworks.com). These should be bite-size videos that explain one feature or service at a time. Let your customer work through several, short videos at their own pace. That is much better than having a potential customer abandon a longer video half way through. Customer testimonials are another effective use of videos. If you have customers who are willing, then videotape them talking about how your product has made their life better.

AUDIO, like radio and the podcast, is not dead! Lots of people like to download podcasts and listen to them on the train or while they are jogging or driving in their car. Podcasts are often great for that purpose because they can be done while the listener has their focus split between listening and driving. Podcasts are great for collaborating with other companies through partnerships or even getting feedback from your clients. Look at RisetotheTop. com for a company built purely on interviews (both in video form and podcasts). DB2 Expert is another example of a company that makes excellent use of podcasts to stay in touch with their user base and demonstrate their expertise.

FILLING OUT YOUR CONTENT

If you find that your site doesn't have much content, you might want to take another look. Are there interesting things you've left out? Are there pictures that might be fun to add? You don't want to clutter your site, but adding content that gives more information about your product or business will enrich the experience and understanding of your customers. Sarah's fishing store provides not only photos and descriptions of the products they sell, but they also have a page dedicated to videos that demonstrate how to use some of their products. Recently Sarah realized that many of her customers asked her about new products. So now she lists the newest products to come out each season on a separate page on the website.

Find out what your customers want. Do they want good customer support after they've purchased a product? Do they want to see examples of your work prior to hiring you? Do they want to get a feel for your location before they book a reservation? Do they want to know what the new fashions are for fall? Don't guess, ask them, and then make sure your website provides this information. The more helpful your website, the more inclined a customer is to come in to your store or contact you directly.

WEBSITE DESIGN

All of this content needs to be tied together by site design. The main purpose of the design is to get out of the way of the content, so people can quickly and easily find what they need on your site. The best thing to do is to focus on creating killer content and keep the design simple.

When looking to design a new website you can hire someone or you can do it yourself. Chances are either way you'll end up using a website design tool like WordPress (also known as a content management system). There are many different types of site builders and you should check them all out, but WordPress is a popular one and that's good. You'll want something that many designers understand and work with and you'll also want something that is user friendly enough for you to use and make changes to.

REUSING CONTENT ON FACEBOOK AND EMAIL

As you work on filling out your website with information, photos, and videos, you are already on your way to enhancing or starting your other social sites. All of the content that you create for your site should be shared with your customers on Facebook (or other social networking sites, like Pinterest and Instagram) or through email.

Imagine the Bar Harbor inn's website. It will focus on all the basics of the inn including photos, information about yearly events, and prices. It should also keep current, perhaps by posting pictures of the seasonal changes of the nearby national park, activities that current guests are enjoying, and a monthly calendar of events in town.

FACEBOOK

Facebook is an excellent way of sharing new content with your fans. The most powerful types of posts are pictures and short videos. Fans can easily browse this type of content directly on Facebook while scrolling through their feed without making a major investment of time and energy, going to your site, or opening your email. Even better, if your fan is in a picture you post to Facebook (perhaps in the follow-up to an event), it will organically be shared with your fan's friends. For example, the inn can post a picture their guests took at the top of a nearby mountain or of the local Fourth of July fireworks show.

Another example: Sara's fishing business had an event where she invited her customers to check out the season's best new equipment. She then ran a raffle where one customer got to go home with a brand new fishing pole! A picture of a smiling customer with his winnings makes for an excellent post to Facebook (hopefully tag the customer too!).

EMAIL

Email is a powerful way of staying in touch with your customers. Much of the content outlined in this chapter can be used in your emails. For example, the Bar Harbor inn sends out a monthly email to its guests. The email contains pictures of Bar Harbor and Acadia National Park as the seasons change, stories of guests on their adventures in Maine, and news about upcoming events in and around Bar Harbor. Please note that nothing that goes on Facebook or email is a direct sales pitch. Instead, you're providing extra value to your customers and fans by giving them exciting information, pictures and videos about topics you already know they are interested in.

REAL WORLD APPLICATION

Michelle makes video demo reels. Dancers and dance studios buy these demos to showcase past performances when auditioning or submitting work to festivals. She has a website which lists her prices and has examples of her past work. She has a consistent, though small, customer base and is thinking about how to expand. She wants a new way of reaching new customers.

In today's age of Facebook, Twitter and email, sharing an article with your friends or colleagues only takes one click. Therefore, the trick for Michelle is to come up with something that is readily shareable, so her existing fans and customers will voluntarily share her brand with their friends.

Michelle thought about all of her dancer friends who had asked her a similar question: what can I do to make my demo reel more interesting? Michelle thought a big problem was that all dancers put two main types of performances on their reel: practicing in a dance studio and performing on a stage. This was getting boring for the dance companies looking to hire dancers. Michelle thought the best and easiest way to spice up a demo reel is to have the dancer perform somewhere else, like a rooftop, a boardwalk, or a basketball court; in short, anywhere other than the same old dance studio and small theater.

So Michelle decided to write a post called the "Top 5 Places to Shoot Your Demo Reel" that she could share on her website and on Facebook, and included pictures of vides and dancers in these locations.

MAKING IT WORK FOR YOU

Give an example of each type of content you can create for your website:

- Writing _____

  _____

- Pictures _____

  _____

- Video _____

  _____

- Audio _____

  _____

In two sentences describe how your website best serves your customers. Then write out which of the above content types best support this. For example, a restaurant focusing on farm to table has customers interested in knowing where their food comes from and how it's farmed, transported and prepared. Therefore, a website rich in photographs and text would be best.

_____

_____

_____

_____

BOTTOM LINE

Your customers want to learn about your business or product long before they ever talk to you. They will do so by consuming the content you produce for your website, Facebook, or email blast. This is your chance to educate your (potential) customers about what you do, how it will make their lives better, and how much it will cost. The more compelling the content the more likely you are to win that person's business.

TOM'S RECORD LABEL

WRITING : Lists of upcoming shows, lyrics, and descriptions of products

PICTURES : Official pictures from concerts, "fanpix," and pictures of products

VIDEOS : Official and fan videos from shows/performances

AUDIO : Songs, interviews from radio

All of this content can be heavily used on social media sites like Facebook.

JANE'S PET SHOP

WRITING : Jane has an extensive background in animal education, training and care. She made sure to include this on her bio page online. One page is simply a list of links to other services in her area that might be of use to her customers. She has write-ups on what she calls Dog Basics; everything an owner should know about the products a puppy, adult and older dog needs. She also has a section called "Happy Pooch, Happy Owner," where she focuses on creating the best possible life for your furry friend. And of course, Jane has an informational page that tells people about her business and why she chose that area of town to open a store. She wants people to feel that she is a part of the neighborhood and to support her small company.

PICTURES : Jane's website has a page devoted to her canine friends. Any photo she's taken for her store's wall of fame also ends up on the website.

VIDEO : Whenever Jane hosts an event at her store she films the event and posts it on her website's video page—that way people who missed an educational event can learn about the topic they were interested in. And new visitors (potential customers) to her website can see she is much more than just a pet store. She has a thriving community and expert knowledge too. Jane also films educational topics, so people can see how best to use the new "Furminator" brush or teach their dog to sit.

AUDIO : Jane hosts a monthly podcast with other local pet experts to discuss both local news that affects her community and more general pet care topics. She archives all these podcasts so when people want to catch up they can look through the older podcasts.

CHAPTER 03
EMAIL
MARKETING

Sally just missed her favorite band, The Shins, when they were in town last week. Sally is your typical over-worked urbanite who loves hanging out with her friends and goes out most weekends. She's not the type of person who is good at keeping up with what's new in the city and although she loves music, she gets too busy to follow her favorite bands' schedules. She relies on her friends to learn about upcoming concerts, but is often disappointed to hear about them *after* tickets have gone on sale and all the good seats are gone or the show is sold out!

What if your clients are like Sally? Chances are they actually *want* someone to tell them about new events, products or services. People want to know more about things they like and if they chose to give their email to your business, chances are they want to hear from you! If your clients are like Sally, and there is a good chance they are, you should be sending them this information about your products and services.

Back to Sally...she finally got herself on the mailing lists for The Shins and three more of her favorite bands. She even paid extra in some cases to be on the VIP list of fans, receiving emails with the chance to buy tickets before they are open to the general public. She's excited to get the emails in the first place. They give her inside information she used to have to seek out on her own. But now it's like having a personal assistant who is helping to keep her in the know.

Your emails should do that for your customers! Here is how they can.

TAKEAWAYS

- Your customer database is the cornerstone of your business.

- Email has the best bang for your buck out of every tool in this book.

- Email campaigns create a relationship with your customers.

- In the world of email campaigns, good content is king.

YOUR EMAIL DATABASE

A strong customer database is the most important digital marketing tool¬ for your business. Anyone who has come to an event, made a purchase, or otherwise interacted with your company should be in it. You can keep this information in an online email database, in an Excel spreadsheet, or in other information sorting software.

Most of the online tools you'll use for email campaigns allow you to use their site to collect this information and then later download it to your computer or transfer the information to another program or site.

> **NOTE:** Make sure to ask everyone you want to add to your list if it is okay to do so. Not only is it the law, it is also the right thing to do.

You will want to add further details about your customers and contacts to your database. For example, if you are a band, you might want to know in what city and state each person resides. Then you can be sure to focus on those people when you tour through their area. You might also want to know which customers have made purchases in the last year and who has made multiple purchases. Details that may be important to keep track of are the date, amount and type of purchase, pages visited on your website, visits to a store, geography and almost anything else that describes your customers' demographic. Then, when you choose to send an email blast to your customers, you can be specific and get the most out of communicating with them.

REAL WORLD APPLICATION

Sarah is a shoe designer in New York. She runs her online store out of her apartment and rents space at a few local shoe stores. Sarah's shoes are different than most in that she only designs shoes in sizes 11 and higher. Sarah uses her email list to do more than just let her customers know when there's a sale. She also uses it to ask them what they want. Surveys are a great way to find out what your customers need and want. Once every season Sarah identifies the newest, hottest trends and puts together an email survey of ten possible designs. She asks customers to choose their three favorites and she also offers a 20% discount if they pre-order a shoe she decides to make. Sarah's customers are not the general population, but they have spent countless hours shopping for shoes without finding anything they like. With Sarah, they never even have to leave the house. They leave it up to her to keep them in style and comfort. They appreciate the quality of the emails she sends and the thought she puts into "why and when" to send an email. Customers feel like each email is from a personal designer writing just to them.

GETTING AN EMAIL FROM YOUR COMPANY

When one of your customers gets an email from your company, you want them to feel that it holds something special. The worst thing you can do is make your customers feel that you're crowding their in-box with unnecessary emails. So how do you make sure it's worth their while? Frequency, design and content, and even more carefully-focused content.

EMAIL FREQUENCY

Know your customers.

Know if it's best to send out an email blast weekly, monthly or only when something special is happening. For example, if you are a band, make sure your fans know when and where you'll be playing next. Or if you sell vintage bags and the holidays are coming up, let your customers know about the top five gifts they can purchase at your online store. Some companies and products require more frequent contact with customers. If you run an email newsletter about hot discount designer sales, you may need to send out daily emails (much like UrbanDaddy or Daily Candy).

While sending email more often than necessary is bad, waiting so long that your customers forget who you are isn't good either. You might want to sit down and look at your yearly (or monthly) schedule of events, holidays, and product releases before planning your emails, or at least have a basic idea of when you'll want to be sending emails out. Then you can plan properly.

It is also possible to ask your customers if they'd like to be emailed weekly or daily, or if they prefer emails about sales, product information, or the latest industry trends. Offering customers a choice can make sure they get exactly the amount of information they want when they want it.

Get specific and really customize your timing and content to your customers' needs.

If you have a database with specific information, you might want to send different email campaigns to different customer groups. You'll have your preferred customers who get information on special events and in-store private sales. You might have customers who only want information on new products and sales. In short, ask your customers for their preferences and then give them what they want.

REAL WORLD QUESTION

In the class we teach at the 3rd Ward in NYC, we got the following question:

"If we're supposed to be unique, send great, relevant content and not email too often, then why do some large chain stores send out the same sale info every single day? Why don't the big guys do what you're teaching us to do?"

Well, the reason is because they are large super chains! These stores are built on a mass-marketing, mass-everything platform. They're in every mall, every magazine and yes, in your inbox every day. If you decide to cancel your email, no big deal, there are a thousand other people signing up for the newsletter the same day. The large chain stores are interested in reaching more people, even if it means each email can't be as high in quality.

You aren't in the same position. You want your customers to love your business and to look forward to receiving your emails. So you need to spend more time thinking carefully about the content your customers want to receive and how often they want to receive it. You need to figure out how often you can send out your emails before they

EMAIL DESIGN

There are many different online email tools that you can use. They all work well, so the best place to start is to look at a few different ones and see which one you prefer. Here are a few of the most popular ones:

- Mail Chimp
- Vertical Response
- Constant Contact
- iContact
- Reverbnation (for independent musicians)

Each of these services offer templates that make your email blast easy to create, as well as more sophisticated email creation tools. You don't want something that looks cookie cutter. With a little time spent reviewing the tutorials each site offers, you'll be able to create something that's professional, polished and includes pictures and videos to enhance the reader's experience.

CONTENT FOR EMAIL

Or rather, CONTENT, CONTENT, CONTENT!!

It is essential that you give the subscribers to your email list something of value. Your customers opened your email—make it worth their while. Make them glad they did and make them want to open the next email you send.

Content is the most important part of your email campaign. Just remember that this is the equivalent to sending someone a letter in the mail. Make sure they are rewarded for opening it and seeing what you have to offer! Look at your own email inbox. Which mailing lists are you on? Which emails do you delete before opening and which ones do you always open? Why? The trick is to take your email campaign and turn it into something that does not look like sales and marketing. Use it as a tool that enhances customer experience.

CALL TO ACTION

A Call to Action is usually a button or link in the email that lets customers know What-To-Do-Next. Start by considering what your email is designed to do. Some common actions are *offering* customers a new product, asking them to subscribe to a newsletter or to come to an event. Your customers need to know exactly what you want them to do with this information.

If you want your customer to make a purchase, then you should put a big button that says "Buy Now" in the email. When they click on the link it will lead them to the page where they can make a purchase. When you see a button that says "Buy Now" you know exactly what to do. If you want your customer to come to a great free event at your store, tell them to "Sign Up Now."

Know what you want the person on the other end of your email to do and make it really clear how they should do it. A useful online resource for testing call to actions is Unbounce.com. We also recommend the book *Don't Make Me Think* by Steve Krug. (This, and all other books we recommend, can be found at ericmorrow.com/books).

REAL WORLD APPLICATION

Jonathan owns a music store that sells a variety of instruments. In his database, he makes sure to include pertinent information about his clients, including what instruments they play. This information lets him single out his guitar-playing customers when any company releases a new guitar. He can even send specific discounts to customers when new accessories come out for an instrument they've already purchased from him (including a call to action). He likes to mix up these email campaigns along with special event notices that he sends to all his customers. This way they know that an email from him in their inbox is either information about a cool music event they'll want to know about or a hot new tip on the latest product that they might actually want or need.

SUBJECT LINES

You can deliver the best content in the world, but if the subject lines of your emails aren't good, your emails will never be opened. Subject lines are the first thing your customer sees when your email arrives in their inbox; they'll decide if they want to read your email based on this line. Subject lines should be straightforward and tell the customer what they'll find inside your email. They should be of medium length and easily readable from a smartphone screen.

When the dance studio writes to their customer list, a good subject line could be "Hot Latin dance party Saturday from 7-10, bring a friend" or "Advanced salsa lessons now on Tuesdays and Thursdays from 6-8". Both of these subject lines clearly state what the reader will find in the email. Avoid subject lines like "News from the dance studio" or "FREE CLASSES NEXT WEEK!" The first is bland and non-descriptive and the second is bland *and* annoying too!

ANALYTICS

Email services also give you useful information about how your email blasts are performing. You can see how many people opened your last email blast. You can even see who clicked on the links within your email. This information can help you learn which types of emails your customers are interested in receiving and which types of emails make them want to click through to see your website or Facebook page. You'll want to see if sending the email out at a different time or with a different subject line makes a difference. With analytics, you learn what's most effective.

BOTTOM LINE

Email is a powerful tool to connect directly with your customers. There are many sites that offer great services for your email campaigns. Each one has extensive tutorials available to help you build the best email campaign possible. Know what your customers want and what it is that makes your company special, before sending your first email.

MAKING IT WORK FOR YOU

List three good reasons to send an email blast to your database.

Examples: information on an upcoming event, a surprise sale

1. _____

2. _____

3. _____

TOM'S RECORD LABEL

Tom primarily sends emails when he has a concert coming up. So he targets a particular geography and sends people living in that area an email before the concert, inviting them to see the show.

Tom also sends emails for big events, like releasing a new CD or music video. These emails go to his entire mailing list, because it is relevant to everyone on his list.

Tom always reaches out to his mailing list at least once a month because there is always at least one exciting thing to talk about! However, if there is only one thing to talk about, he keeps the email to just that one thing. Pretending to have exciting things going on doesn't work—his readers are smarter than that.

JANE'S PET SHOP

Jane knows her customers and their pets quite well from their frequent visits to her store. She respects their time and only send them emails with information she is sure they will be interested in. Because of this respect and value-add, her customers are happy to sign up for her email lists.

She sends out emails for three main reasons:

1. Once a month when there is a special, free event at the store such as a workshop on trimming pets' nails.

2. Four times a year to announce her quarterly sale.

3. Once a year on the pet's birthday. She keep track of the birthdays of all her clients' pets and sends out a special birthday discount to each of them.

CHAPTER 04
SOCIAL MEDIA

Julia is a personal trainer. She had a website where she advertised her services and her prices. She knew Facebook was important and wanted to get on it. So the first thing she did was copy her list of services and prices onto her Facebook page and asked her friends and clients to "Like" it. Now she had 20 likes but no one was coming to visit her page or read her posts.

Julia saw that other personal trainers were developing a following on their pages—she wanted to know what was different. As she started looking more closely at successful Facebook pages, she noticed that they did not focus on their services and prices. Some did have a listing of these on additional pages, but many simply used a link to their website for this information. They used their Facebook pages as a tool for another function.

Julia found that most successful exercise Facebook pages created a place where, for example, fitness clients could discuss different exercises, swap recipes for healthy and delicious cooking, and share videos and articles about, not surprisingly, fitness!

Julia first tried to use Facebook to sell her services. This didn't create any new value or reason for people to visit her page or like her posts. Now Julia is focused on creating a fun environment for her customers to talk about fitness and share their lifestyle. She does this by posting pictures of the healthy food she cooks (along with recipes), sharing interesting articles and posting videos of fun exercises. This creates a community of like-minded people who all share the same interests.

"Social" (aka social media) is not a place to sell. It should be used as a place to share your original content, get feedback from customers, and generally create a lively community of people using your product or service.

TAKEAWAYS

- Don't sell on social media.
- Create a community.
- Bring your fans inside your process.
- Tell your story, show some personality.

SOCIAL MEDIA TOOLS

When we talk about "social," we mean Facebook, Twitter, LinkedIn, Pinterest, Instagram and every other social space on the Internet. Social is a tool that allows people to communicate with one another. Facebook, Twitter, phone calls, email, and text messages are all tools that allow people to connect with one another.

These tools all help people to communicate in different ways. If you wanted to get long, detailed information to a friend about an upcoming trip, you would email it to them rather than text it. This is because of the amount of the material involved and how it's most useful for them to receive it. You want to apply the same logic to all of your online tools.

People use social sites to talk with their friends, share pictures, watch videos, discover interesting articles, and just about anything else you can imagine! Social sites mirror people's lives and what they are interested in. That makes it especially important that you, as a business, tread gently in this space. Just as you don't hand out flyers for your business at a party, don't plaster marketing messages all over your social media efforts. Social sites are not sites you should use to sell your product.

One specific characteristic of social sites is that they are many-to-many communication tools.

Social tools, like blogs and Facebook, allow many people to talk to many other people simultaneously, similar to a town hall meeting. Many people can speak, many people can be heard, and many types of collaboration can take place. This type of interaction is very important for both growing the community of your customers as well as learning about them. Social is the only place you can build and foster your community and then sit back and study your customers. If you create a place where your customers can openly discuss your products with one another, there is much to learn.

FEEDBACK

Feedback is where customer service begins. Your clients (or customers) can tell you what they liked about your product or service and what they disliked. Software development relies heavily on this feedback. Rather than companies developing software and features they think their clients might want, clients can tell companies what they want and play an active role in the development of the software—then the clients get exactly what they need.

Feedback can apply to any business type or model. And it won't always be positive! Positive feedback is clearly a sign that you're doing something right as a business. But even doing something wrong is okay - social gives you quick feedback when you do something wrong so that you can correct course and better please your customers.

An example of this might be as simple as someone posting on your help and support forums that they had an issue with a product. By responding to this post promptly with a solution, you make sure they have a good experience with your product or service. Plus, if other people have the same problem, you don't need to fix it one at a time. Now everyone in your community knows how to solve this particular issue.

Or take the example of a customer writing to ask why you don't offer a particular service. If many other customers comment that they too would gain from this service you would learn right away how to grow your business. If you're looking to grow your business in a certain area why not post this on Facebook and ask for feedback. It could help in taking the guesswork out of future business decisions. There is a growing startup scene called "Lean Startup" that revolves around the principle of letting your customers guide your business growth. (Learn more about Lean Startup here: http://en.wikipedia.org/wiki/Lean_Startup).

SHARING

Everyone wants his or her video to go viral. Going viral means people are actively and willfully sharing your video (probably with your message in it) with their social networks. Going viral means you've created something so interesting that people feel compelled to share it, of their own volition.

But viral isn't the only mechanism for sharing—that's just when sharing "tips" to become a massive amount of shares between friends. Sharing is also an important marketing mechanism even at the smaller end of the scale. Everything that occurs online can be shared, from a story about excellent (or terrible) customer service, to clever marketing videos like ads, good music, trailers, excerpts from books, and useful information on how to load your dishwasher. Sharing starts with good content.

Figuring out what types of posts get shared is easy. Check out other sites online and see which of their posts received the most likes and comments. Check out the Facebook, Pinterest and Twitter pages for your competitors. See what is working for them. Check out your favorite Facebook pages and ask yourself what it is about them you like. Or simply pay attention to the type of posts you actually click on or share with others on a daily basis. Chances are that a humorous top ten list far surpasses a 10% off coupon.

500 PASSIONATE CUSTOMERS = BUSINESS!

Facebook allows you to create a very personal connection with each of your customers. Overall, social is a powerful way to make sure you are keeping your customers happy. You can ask them how they liked your product or service and if they want any improvements. Social should serve as the foundation of a feedback loop between the customer and the business. A small company doesn't need an unlimited number, or even that big of a number, of customers to survive and thrive. It just needs a passionate customer base that can best be maintained using social tools. If you can find 500 people who would each pay $100 a year for your product or service, you're in business!!

CONTENT

Once you start thinking of social as a way to connect with your customers, and not a way to sell to them, then you can start using social as a tool to get feedback and promote sharing. This is all done through providing good content. Content that is relevant to your customers is the key.

For Facebook there are two main areas to address. The first is your cover image. The cover image should be reflect your business. Does your business sell cameras that capture extreme sports? Make a collage of the craziest photos your customers have sent you. Your business is exciting: make sure your customer gets that sense from the first moment their eyes see your Facebook page. If you sell cupcakes, make sure your most unique ones are the first thing a visitor sees. A yoga instructor might include a popular pose or a photo of one of their popular outdoor classes. Make sure to use good, clear captivating images that let your customers know exactly the personality of your business.

The second area of content is the Facebook timeline, where you can share and highlight your most memorable posts, photos and events. Any content you develop for your website or email blasts are fair game for Facebook posts—that means videos, podcasts, pictures, and articles can be good content to share with your fans via Facebook. While much of the content you create for your website should be original, content for Facebook can go beyond that. Social content can be more casual and in the moment. You can share posts from other Facebook pages, interesting articles from news sites, or funny posts from blogs. When you look at a successful Facebook page, it doesn't feel formal. It feels like someone is talking directly to you as a friend.

Know your business's personality and let it shine. The timeline is the place to add layers to your business. You can let your customers get to know you. Look on Facebook at some of the celebrities who have a strong fan base. See that they aren't selling themselves. Their fans know that they can go to their website for information on performances and products. They go to Facebook to get a more personal interaction. For some celebrities their fans are thrilled to know some of the simplest things about them that make them seem more human and accessible.

For a nutritionist, you might find descriptions of meals, shopping lists and supplements on their website. This information can also be good content for Facebook, but it would be posted in a much more personal and timely manner. "Wow, it's strawberry season and I just bought the best strawberries at my local farmer's market!" Or post a picture of the biggest pumpkin grown this season.

Go online and see what other businesses like yours are posting. See what your friends are talking about. You know best what are the hot trends in your area of expertise. Comment on them from your businesses point of view.

When looking for ways to express your personality and present your content, don't underestimate the power of images. Instagram is one of the most popular social tools and it is nothing more than images posted in a timeline. An image is not only a simple and powerful way to get a point across, it's also fun and easy to repost. If you sell antiques, chances are that your customers are passionate about antiques they own and find as well. They would much rather see a photo of a newly restored phonograph than read about it. A makeup artist works in a visual media. She might be touting her new lipstick line, but her Facebook page should be filled with images of her makeup in action, or the coolest makeup trends of the season. Try expressing whatever you find most interesting with an image whenever possible.

FREQUENCY

Frequency on social media is how often you write or post. You want to post on a "regular basis." Knowing your customers will help to answer the question of what that means. If you own a coffee shop, you have customers interested in coffee at different times of the day, early morning, afternoon and maybe even after work. If your clients are stay-at-home moms maybe they're on the computer during naptimes, but not after work hours when it's time for dinner and bedtime routines. Know your customers and you'll know when to post. And if you can't figure it out, ask them when they check-in to the digital world.

Facebook posting frequency is different than the frequency of sending an email to your customers. When you send an email it sits in their inbox until they choose to deal with it by either opening it or deleting it. With Facebook, the timeline is always updating. That means if you post something at 11 am, and many of your customers don't go online until 3 pm, then they may not see your post. You might find that you're more effective sending the same information in 2-3 creative and different ways throughout a day.

Or if you're promoting an event you might want to post something new about the event every day. With Facebook you can tell if your posts are effective by seeing how many people *Like* or *Share* your link. Conversely, if customers start removing themselves from your page, you're doing something wrong. Don't be afraid to experiment and see what works.

More important is the speed at which you respond to your customers' posts. If they ask a question, you should answer it immediately. If they post something positive, "Like" it on Facebook or thank them on Twitter. Social is a conversation. Try and keep it going. In the preceding paragraphs about cover image and timeline there was a lot of emphasis on letting your customer know you. Don't forget that this is also the **BEST** way to get to know your customer. Facebook and Twitter are great places to learn about your customers. So make sure to read what your customers post on your page and on their pages. And don't forget to look at other businesses and people's feeds. There's a whole conversation going on out there. Don't miss it.

MAKING IT WORK FOR YOU

What are three things you can do on social media besides selling your product?

1. _____

2. _____

3. _____

BOTTOM LINE

People are more interconnected today than ever before. Social media sites like Facebook and nearly ubiquitous smartphones allow people to talk directly with each other and the businesses they buy from instantly. Participating in social media is a must for any business. People frequently turn to Facebook long before they walk into your store or check out your site. When they do so, they should find a thriving community of your customers.

TOM'S RECORD LABEL

Tom built his customer base on Facebook and MySpace. Many small businesses add customers one at a time and Tom was no different. He started by writing and recording some music and playing it at very small shows. He made his music available online and shared it with people he thought would like it (primarily by looking at other musical artists people said they liked). He worked hard to develop a personal connection with each person who enjoyed his music and he still does the same thing these days.

People like Tom's music because they like Tom. So Tom makes himself accessible, in large part through Facebook. Tom uses Facebook a few hours each day, to post pictures and funny comments from his tour, and exchange messages with his fans.

Social is a tool that Tom makes great use of, but it isn't the end result. Tom doesn't use Facebook so he can *say* he uses Facebook. His goal is to connect with his customers and create a community of people who love his music.

JANE'S PET SHOP

Jane knows that her customers love their pets. She built her online community around her role as being the expert on what products and services are the best for their pets. Her Facebook page reflects this in her posts about new and interesting products. However, most of her page is devoted to pictures of her furry customers. She posts pictures of the pets that come into her shop, cute pictures of animals she finds online, and re-posts of other pet lovers' posts. When you go to her page you find many cute pictures of animals that her followers frequently *Like* and *Share*. *Liking* and *Sharing* a photo is something easy and people tend to do it with photos of cute animals.

Also, if someone asks her a question online she makes sure to reply promptly with an educated and well-informed answer. She always puts in the work to give a good answer.

In the world of blogging, Jane has shared her expertise by writing many blog posts about high-end dog products. She is a weekly guest blogger for a popular online pet blog as well as many blogs for online magazines about dogs.

CHAPTER 05
ONLINE
CONVERSATIONS

Imagine you're in a new part of town. You're meeting your friend for coffee and they text you to say, "I'm hungry, can you choose a place to meet where we can get something to eat?" This is good because you're hungry too. You've actually been thinking about having that perfect slice of pizza all day. What's the first thing you do? Ten years ago you might have called a friend who lives in the area, asked someone in the coffee shop you're sitting in (to see if they know the neighborhood), looked in the Yellow Pages or just left early and drove around to see if anything looked good.

Today things are a little different. The impulse hasn't changed, but now you just pull out your smart phone and do a quick search for Italian restaurants in the area. Suppose you discover there are two Italian restaurants nearby. How do you choose? Lucky for you, others have already visited and reviewed these restaurants. The Brick Oven sounds like a good match for your craving, but then you see that most viewers gave it a 2-3 out of 5 stars, said it was more like a fast food environment and that it wasn't clean. On the other hand, another restaurant, Max's, received 5 stars for most of their ratings. They are said to have a casual and comfortable environment, perfect for catching up over a glass of wine and a yummy Italian dish. A quick view of their menu shows that they have several pasta dishes and even a few pizzas you'd like to try. Your decision is made. Armed with this information, you text your friend the restaurant information, Google Map the address, and your plans are set.

TAKEAWAYS

- People decide if they want to buy your product or service before they ever set foot in your store or meet you in person.
- Use the feedback you get online to improve.

Customers are now looking online for information about companies more than ever before. (Google calls this the Zero Moment of Truth - ZeroMomentOfTruth.com). Being knowledgeable about your online presence and being responsive to customer's questions and concerns has never been more important. Your existing and potential customers are online looking for information about products and services and you need to know how they search for information and what they are learning about your business.

Online conversation and reviews should be an exciting and helpful tool for you in many ways. You are now privy to the word on the street about your business. You don't have to wonder what your reputation is because you can see it online. What's more, you can see what people like about your company and you can use this information to make changes when and where they are needed.

Start by doing your research. Find out where your business is being listed, reviewed or discussed online. You can start by doing a general search of the various popular search engines online. Try searching for your company the way one of your customers would search.

There are many ways people search for information on the Internet. Here are some examples:

- Google, Bing (general search engine)
- Yelp, OpenTable (restaurants)
- eBay, Craigslist, StubHub, Amazon (goods marketplace)
- Airbnb, VRBO, Homeaway, Wimdu (accommodations)
- TripAdvisor, Kayak, Travelocity, Thorntree, Hotwire (travel)
- Rotten Tomatoes (movies)

Regardless of what you're interested in buying, you can find information on pricing, location, and quality online in an instant.

REVIEWS

Reviews are a standard part of the decision-making purchase process these days. And it isn't just review-oriented sites like Yelp and Consumer Reports. Amazon and many stores include reviews right on the item's description page. Customer reviews are a great way to see what other people, probably your peers, think about a restaurant, a movie, a hotel or the latest digital camera.

However, reviews aren't always neatly aggregated in a highly searchable way. Many sites operate as a forum - like ThornTree - lonelyplanet.com/thorntree or GardenWeb - ths.gardenweb.com/forums. Although not as easily shareable and sortable as other sites, forums are still a dominant way people on the internet share information with each other.

GOOGLE ALERTS

Since the internet is a very big place, Google conveniently offers a free service that lets you know when a certain keyword (like the name of your business or product) is used anywhere on the web: google. com/alerts. Setting up a Google Alert is a simple way to stay up to date on who is talking about you and your business and where they are talking about it. And because it alerts you whenever a new listing or comment is posted about your company (or whatever keyword you select), you can stay on top of what people are saying.

MAKING YOUR ONLINE PRESENCE RESPONSIVE TO REVIEWS

Once you have done your research, you should have a clear idea of what your online presence is like (outside of your own website). Now you can start taking steps towards having the online con-versation work for you. You'll want to build your online presence, improve your online reviews and ratings and use this information as a way to improve your business.

First, take note of where people are talking about you online and encourage your customers to review your business. One way to do this is to simply ask your customers to go online and write a review of your product or service. When you send out your next email news-letter, try including the link to a popular review site and encourage people to comment.

Don't forget to notice the places online where people *should* be talking about your business but aren't. For example, if you own a cupcake shop, are you listed on the popular restaurant sites? Does your business show up when you search on Google Maps? If your business isn't listed, contact those sites and find out how to include it.

REAL WORLD APPLICATION

In Atlanta, a full-time mother named Jennifer owned a small business where she baked vegan and gluten-free desserts. She started baking these desserts because her own children were allergic to various dairy and wheat products and she couldn't find sweets that both tasted good and met her children's dietary needs. Her clients all agreed that her desserts tasted just as good as the real thing. Jennifer went online and saw that although she had a strong client base, made up of diet-restricted moms and their kids, she only had one or two reviews on most of the store and restaurant review sites.

She decided to ask every customer to go online and write a review. When they would check out she'd say, "If you have an extra minute, next time you're online I'd love it if you could write a review on Yelp!" She started sending a "thank you" email to customers after they made a purchase and asking them to please write a review online. She included a direct link to make it easy for them. By the end of the month she had many new reviews and several of them were detailed and helpful descriptions of the shop, Jennifer's unique desserts and her helpful service. Now people searching for vegan desserts had more information about her shop available when they were choosing a place to order their next cake.

HOW TO APPROACH THE NEGATIVE REVIEW

When you come across a bad review don't get discouraged. While the vast majority of online reviews are positive, people like to talk about their experiences, and since we live in the real world, mistakes happen—which means you'll eventually get some bad reviews. If the service and products are great then people are happy and frequently express their thanks online. But for the inevitable bad experience, the internet provides customers a convenient place to air their complaints.

A bad review should be seen as a chance to turn an unhappy customer into a happy customer. The worst case is that after one bad experience the customer will turn around and tell their friends and family about your company and you won't have a chance to do anything to fix the problem. But if this customer goes online to voice their unhappiness, now you know about it, and can address it. You can reach out to the customer and offer to make it right.

Recently a friend had a bad experience at a salon and complained on Yelp. The salon contacted her the next day and invited her to come back in for a manicure *gratis*, as a way to apologize. Even if you can't resolve the problem directly, at least let the reviewer know they were heard and you're doing everything you can to improve that aspect of your business. You can even thank them for their constructive comments.

What you should never do is get defensive! Bad experiences happen—defensive reactions don't have to. Accept that you didn't meet the customer's expectations and try to fix the problem. Of course, not every customer's problem can be resolved. In those cases, learn what you can from the experience and try not to repeat it in the future.

Most importantly, how many of your reviews are positive or negative? One negative review and ten positive ones make you more real. You run a company in the real world and mistakes happen. But someone reading your reviews can readily see that most people who frequent your business leave happy.

Some sites, like ResellerRatings and Yelp, provide an easy way for business owners to respond to customer questions, concerns and complaints. Other sites, like GardenWeb, are forums where consumers talk directly to each other and the voice of a business is treated just like any other voice (albeit with something to sell).

The best way to deal with your online business presence is to be honest, helpful, and to not try and sell anything. Encourage customers to comment on your business and take note of what's being said when they do.

INTEGRATING REVIEWS WITH YOUR ONLINE SALES

Reviews about your overall business are very helpful to you, but you can also turn the world of reviews and comments into a tool for your customers. Let's say you sell custom home stereo systems. On your site, you might have past customers commenting on the speakers they purchased. In this way you are allowing possible new customers to get information on your services as well as on the product itself. Now Joe is online looking to purchase new speakers for his living room. He sees several photos of speakers other customers have purchased. He can see the specifications they chose and also read about how those customers are enjoying the speakers in their homes. He'll learn that your company delivered the product ontime and was helpful in the design process, and that most of the people who purchased a certain type of speaker were very happy with the sound in their large living rooms. You can turn your past customers into reviewers of your products to help you win new customers.

BOTTOM LINE

Making decisions can be difficult. No matter the situation, the more information a person has and the more sources that information comes from—the better. Make sure the reviews people read about you are positive.

MAKING IT WORK FOR YOU

What are the top three sites where people talk about your product or service?

1. _____

2. _____

3. _____

TOM'S RECORD LABEL

Tom's music is most frequently talked about on his Facebook page. But Tom also can see where people are talking more generally about music (or music by gay musicians) at sites like MTV's Logo. Tom's albums are often reviewed on sites like CD Baby. If you view Tom's music on YouTube, many other people have left comments about what they think of his songs.

For independent, creative people like Tom (and you), a lot of reviews will come in the form of blog posts from other people; some people who hear Tom's music write blog posts about how it makes them feel.

JANE'S PET SHOP

When Jane's shop first opened the first thing she did was to make sure it was listed online. She went to Google's Places for Business and listed her shop so that when people looked at Google Maps, her site would pop up. She didn't want to be left out when people did a quick search in her area. She also noticed that when she did an online search most shops had reviews listed on Yelp. After a quick search for "How do I list my business on Yelp" she learned how her business could be listed. Now was the hard part: getting the word out. She started with a few close friends who supported her from the start and had already stopped by the shop several times. Because these people are "big fans" so to speak, they were more than willing to write a review for the shop. Then, when new customers came into the store Jane would note if they were pleased that her store was now in the neighborhood. If they were, she'd say, "I'm glad we're here too! I'd love to stay. Could you help me by writing a review on Yelp?"

CHAPTER 06
EVENTS

Lisa owns a small jewelry shop in the Pacific Heights neighborhood of San Francisco. She just received a new shipment of earrings with dangling pastel colored gemstones. She believes they will be popular with the type of fashionable, young, affluent women who live in Pacific Heights and walk by her store every day. Her problem is that she needs to get these women to stop and come in and browse. She decides to host a "Browse with Bubbles" champagne party and puts a big sign on the street that says "Free Champagne while you browse." Lisa also sends out an invitation to her mailing list and puts a notice on Facebook. And it works! Women walk by the store and see the sign (or see the electronic "signage" in their inbox), and come in to sample the champagne while browsing the jewelry.

TAKEAWAYS

- Add value, don't sell : events should be fun, informative, or tasty and not require anything to be purchased.

- Events get your customers offline so they can interact with you and each other.

- Social : advertise events on Facebook, post pictures after the event.

- Email : notify mailing list before the event.

WHAT IS AN EVENT?

An event is a special real world experience that you host to support your product, brand, and customers. The event gives people reasons to come to your store or gallery that are above and beyond purchasing your product. Your customer should be able to do something at the event that doesn't directly relate to buying your product or service.

EVENTS SHOULD ADD VALUE WITHOUT SELLING

Creating an event doesn't have to be (and often shouldn't be) directly related to the sale of your product. Maybe you're an artist with large paintings and you want to hang them in a fun space and have a local band play with your art as their backdrop. This makes the space more festive and adds to the fans' enjoyment of the music, while at the same time exposing more people to your art.

If you run a wine shop, you can have a free "Wines of Spain" tasting. If you own a café or bookstore, you might have a poetry reading or a live music event. If you run a dance studio, you can have a night of introductory lessons to the different styles you teach or have a party where anyone can come enjoy the music and dance. If you're a personal trainer, you can host a free workout in the park for your students and make it open to all. The options are almost limitless! And all events have the virtue of introducing your product or service to both new and existing customers.

EVENTS HELP DEFINE THE IMAGE AND BRAND OF YOUR COMPANY

Events help to establish your brand/identity. This is a great way to get people to think of your brand and the identity behind it.

If you're a fashion designer with a small store you could host a fashion show. Maybe you partner with a local charity and have friends model your latest designs. You can then auction the clothes that the models were wearing to raise money for the charity. Supporting a local charity with an event involving your business is a good way to create a positive association between your customers and your store or brand. It will also bring in new people to see your designs.

EVENTS CREATE NEW CONTENT

Events create new content for your online world, blog, Facebook, and email marketing. Fresh and exciting content is the best reason for getting in touch with your customer base and showing potential customers what your business is all about. Pictures are both easy to create and share and are interesting to your customers. You can show your customers having fun in your space and with your product. A dog groomer can post pictures of customers with their dogs after a styling consult event or the personal trainer can show pictures of their customers working out at the free event. And of course, invite people to come to the next event!

EVENTS TO REWARD YOUR BEST CUSTOMERS

Events can be a special thank you for your customers and can reinforce your relationship with them. If you have a segment of customers who make large purchases, purchase often, or are special supporters of your work, you want to thank them. You can do this by having an event that selectively invites your best customers. You might want to invite them to be the first to purchase your products during a sale. They might be able to see your new products before the general public. If you have a gallery showing, invite them to the invitation-only pre-party with free drinks and food.

MAKING IT WORK FOR YOU

List two events you could do this month. Start small.

1. _____

2. _____

BOTTOM LINE

Get people off the computer, into your store, and bring your community together. An event should be fun and not require attendees to buy anything. Use social and email to inform people about the event and post follow-ups after the event.

TOM'S RECORD LABEL

The nature of Tom's business is that there are always events! Each concert is an event that helps bring his customers together to enjoy his music. But Tom doesn't stop there. He hosts special concerts as fundraisers for the causes he cares about. He plays at gay marriage rallies. His music and audience is almost tailor-made for events and partnerships. He also invites his audience to participate in the filming of his music videos.

JANE'S PET SHOP

Jane hosts monthly free events at her shop. One month she had an expert groomer come in and demonstrate how to properly wash a dog. Another month she had a dog walker/dog owner mixer. She invited 10 dog walkers from the area to come to the store and meet with dog owners and their pets. She helped pair up dogs of various types with dog walkers who are knowledgeable of those particular breeds.

CHAPTER 07
PARTNERSHIPS

Elise lives in an apartment building in the city, and although she has a lovely neighborhood, she sees mostly the same six blocks that it takes her to walk from her apartment to the subway train. When a new cheese shop moved in four blocks north of her, she didn't even hear about it for six months as she spends most of her free time with friends downtown. Knowing this and knowing that many people are just like Elise, the cheese shop decided to partner up with a wine store in the same neighborhood. During the summer, every Tuesday from 4 pm – 7 pm, when most people are walking home (by the more conveniently located wine shop), the two stores partner up to do a tasting—wine and cheese from around the world! People who come into the store get to try several pairings and sometimes even walk away with a sample to take home. The wine store is happy to have the cheese to make their customers' visit more rewarding. The cheese store is happy to have a chance to introduce its products to the wine store's customers. And the customers are happy because they get to have some wine and cheese.

TAKEAWAYS

- Partnerships are win-win situations.
- Overlapping demographics are essential for successful partnerships.
- Similar demographics, different products.

OVERLAPPING DEMOGRAPHICS

Partnerships are a great way of reaching potential new customers. Your first step in choosing a company for a partner is to look for a business with an overlapping demographic. You don't want a company that sells the same product you do, but you do want a company that sells to the same group of people. This is where it's important to really know your own demographic. For example, if you say your demographic is men and women 18 – 35, that's a very general group. A running shoe company might then think that a company that sells popular music might be a good company to partner with. In some cases this might be a good fit while in others it might not. Not all people ages 18 – 35 enjoy the same type of music.

However, if the same company decided to partner with a company that specializes in pro running socks, that's a much better fit. Not only do the demographics overlap, but the direct needs of the demographics overlap. No matter what other things a person is interested in, if they are purchasing an expensive pair of pro running shoes, the chances that they'll need socks to go with the shoes are very high. It's a great partnership—similar demographics, similar product fields, and no competition between the two companies.

BENEFIT BOTH SIDES

The next step is to make sure that the partnership benefits both companies. In the shoes and socks example this might come in the form of a giveaway. The shoe store wants to make sure that their regular customers have a positive experience. And let's say that the socks company is a fairly new company and does most of its sales online. It wants to introduce its products to more customers. One such partnership that would benefit both companies would be for the shoe store to give away a pair of socks with each purchase for an entire week or month. The store benefits from the added value of giving their customers something extra. The socks company benefits by having the shoe company help connect them with new customers. If the runners like the socks, they will then look to the socks company for future purchases.

Now let's imagine the shoe store was interested in gaining more customers. They might look to partner with a local road race. Again, the demographics cross, but in this case the shoe company would be on the side of adding value to the race. Maybe they put a 25% coupon in the grab bag each runner gets, or a free water bottle with the store logo. Now the race has an added value and the shoe store gains exposure. There are numerous ways to create partnerships. The main point is to know what your company's goals are and seek out a company to partner with, where it makes sense for both sides.

HOW TO FIND A PARTNER

The best ways to start a partnership are to do your homework and to be proactive. First, identify a good company for a partnership. Make sure the other company has an overlapping demographic and that the partnership would benefit both companies. Once you have narrowed down your search to a good company, study them. Learn about what they are currently doing to market themselves. Do they have an online presence? Are they hosting events? What does their store or office look like or where is it located? Then you will want to come up with a good plan. Whether it's to write an article for an upcoming blog post, co-host an event or cross promote in email newsletters, you need to have a few ideas to present to the other company. You will want to have about three solid ideas to present to them when you meet or have that first phone call. Don't just call them and say you want to work with them, call them and have a plan. A plan will show that you are serious, a strong business partner, and that you're a fan of their business.

BE TRUE TO YOUR BRAND

Marketing is about getting your product and your message to potential customers in your demographic. You want them to know about you so when it's time for them to make a purchase they know who you are, where you are, and what they're purchasing. You need to maintain the integrity of your message or brand. Make sure to partner with other companies that also have a similar message or brand. An organic baby food company might see a company that sells organic cookies as a good fit. However, customers in this demographic might see the cookie company's product as un-healthy for kids, even though it is organic. Since the baby food company prides itself on the healthy content of its product, this is not a good partnership. The message they might send is that they don't really care that much about health and nutrition.

ONLINE PARTNERSHIPS

There are many different ways to find a valuable partner online. You'll see many common examples of this when you get email updates, read blogs, and visit various websites.

An easy partnership for the digital era is guest blogging. When you write a guest blog for someone else, it is clear what you are getting—the attention of your blog partner's readers. All blogs needs regular fresh new content that is relevant and interesting to the blog's readers. That is where the guest blogger comes in and a natural partnership is born. The guest blogger produces new content for the blog and adds value for the blog's readers.

Online or offline, partnerships should be all about adding value for your partner and their readers, client, or customers. For example, think of an artist who wants to get noticed and display her artwork. A creative partnership might be with the local wine shop or event space (think outside the normal gallery presentation!) Artwork created for the partner can be displayed and will add value to the space. In exchange, the artist reaches a wider audience, allowing her to take advantage of the audience someone else has already built.

NICHE AND RELEVANT > WIDE AND IRRELEVANT

As we've talked about in this book, reaching a wide audience is good, but reaching a relevant audience is even better. To reach a niche audience, you should understand your demographic and then seek out a business with a complementary, overlapping demographic.

For example, let's say you are in the business of making running apps for smartphones. You are looking for beta testers for your new app. Where could you find your audience? One place is an online forum for runners. Maybe the mainstream apps from Nike and Adidas have some flaws that you can solve for people and you'll learn about these flaws on the forums. Or maybe you need to go offline and create a partnership with a local 5k race or running club. You get access to the right kind of people who would be interested in your product or service and your partner gets to introduce some cool new technology to their audience—a win-win!

The most exciting aspect of partnerships is that they can exist anywhere and require just enough effort that many people aren't taking advantage of them. Start looking for partnerships by finding businesses that serve your demographic and then approach them with a value-add proposition they can't refuse.

BOTTOM LINE

Your product should create value for your partner's demographic and vice versa. A successful partnership is one where both companies feel they have added value to their customers' experience through the partnership. Look for overlapping demographics. Although you don't want to partner with a company selling a similar product, you do want to partner with a company who has customers of a similar demographic.

MAKING IT WORK FOR YOU

Describe a business you could partner with, their demographics, and an event or project you could do with them

_____

_____

_____

_____

_____

_____

_____

TOM'S RECORD LABEL

Tom loves to do partnerships. The one he does almost every night he performs is to have an opening act. He normally tours with other gay musicians who have a similar demographic—middle-aged, gay men who like love songs written by gay men.

Tom also performs at benefits for the causes he believes in. An added bonus is that the people he is playing for are generally new to his music but come from the demographic that tends to like his music. All in all, it's a win-win!

Appearing on a radio show or TV station about gay musicians is another partnership that is very fruitful for Tom. These shows already have audiences that are predisposed to like Tom and his music and they are getting extra value from learning about Tom. And Tom gets to expose new people to his music. The same applies for appearing in newspaper or magazine articles—all win-wins.

JANE'S PET SHOP

Jane knows that there are many other pet businesses in the area. There are groomers, doggie daycares, and trainers. Often she'll pair up with one of these other companies. She's given away coupons to the other businesses for a free doggie toy if the owner stops by her store. She's also partnered up with them to do events. One of her monthly events took place at a neighboring doggie daycare where she treated her clients to an hour with the local dog whisperer.

CHAPTER 08
CURATION

David works at a law school helping students find jobs in public interest careers. Every day he receives emails and newsletters from countless organizations around the United States that have job openings, internships and volunteer opportunities. He also gets updates through his social networks that offer advice on how to best find a job in the public interest world. There is more information out there than any law student could hope to sift through with the limited time they have for job hunting.

As David goes through his emails, newsletters, and social updates, he compiles a list of the most useful and relevant postings and articles. Every week he sends this short list out to his email list and posts it on his blog and social networks. Students at the law school have been signing up for his email distribution so they can stay on top of their job hunt as efficiently as possible. David's blog has also seen tremendous interest and visitors because of his weekly curation efforts. His most recent post on the "Top ten ways to find a job in public interest" was his most popular post ever.

TAKEAWAYS

- Curation : Top ten list

- Highlight what other people like.

- Helpful for people who don't have a lot of experience in your field.

CURATION IS A TOP TEN LIST

If you've ever seen, read, or forwarded a top ten list online, you've seen the results of curation. Top ten lists are great starting points for people new to a topic and they can cover anything and everything. Start typing "Top ten things to consider" into Google and you'll get countless results. No matter your field you can produce a top ten (or five or three) list of things to think about when, for example, hiring a web designer. Or maybe you're an expert in gardening so you produce a top ten list about which tools are best for the rooftop urban gardener.

The purpose of curation is to familiarize people with their options or introduce them to a new topic. Another popular top ten list that you've heard of is the New York Times Bestseller List. A bestseller list is another example of curation, this time by crowdsourcing. If you've ever purchased a bestseller because it was a bestseller, you probably thought, *"If everyone else liked this book, then maybe I will too. It's worth a shot!"*

Perhaps you have purchased a bottle of wine from the "Top Ten wines under $10" bin at your local wine shop. This is another form of curation, this time by the wine shop owner. Unless you're a frequent wine drinker who really knows what you like, there are probably times you've gone into a wine store and wandered around aimlessly for a bit. Maybe during one of these times you've read the description tags attached to a bottle that describe the wine's characteristics or how it was rated by Wine Spectator magazine (another form of curation). Ultimately, you may have picked out a bottle from a "Top Ten" case, maybe of French reds, or best American producers, or most commonly, under $10 or $15. That "Top Ten" case is how the wine shop does curation.

Even something as simple as listening to the radio is a form of curation. The DJ is picking songs to play from an almost infinite number of choices and you're listening to the radio because you trust that DJ's choice. Or maybe you're using Pandora or another internet radio service, in which case you trust a computer algorithm to choose music you'll enjoy.

Rotten Tomatoes is a movie review website. It aggregates individual movie reviews and creates a composite "Tomato" score that describes how good a movie is. And each year they release a top ten list of the best movies of that year. You can see an example from 2010 here: http://www.rottentomatoes.com/guides/golden-tomato-awards-2012/

Regardless of your field, and how much of an expert you think you are in that field, you are almost always going to know more about the field than your customer. Whether it's art, wine, books or cars, you spend each day thinking about that topic; your customer is most likely only thinking about it for five minutes, while they are trying to solve a particular problem. Curation is an excellent way to highlight your expertise and help your customer make a decision about something to buy.

CURATION FOR CONTENT

In the example of law school public interest jobs, where David highlights interesting articles and posts in a weekly blog update, David is creating content for his website. Curation is an effective way of simply creating content for your site that can generate a lot of interest and attract visitors.

CURATION FOR SOCIAL MEDIA

Whenever you repost something on Facebook or retweet something on Twitter, you are curating. And this is the simplest way of getting started! Every day you can post one item to your social media network in your area of expertise. If you're a cupcake maker, your curation efforts may include reposting a magazine's cupcake photo shoot, a birthday party with clever, creative cupcakes, or a recipe for a seasonal cupcake. All of these demonstrate that you are plugged into the cupcake world and are up-to-date. Your customers or fans know when they see posts from you that they will be high quality, interesting and relevant.

MAKING IT WORK FOR YOU

What are things your customers want to know that you can make into a top ten list?

1. _____

2. _____

3. _____

BOTTOM LINE

Your customers come to you for much more than just a finished product or service. They often shop with you because of your expertise in a certain field. Curation, most simply making a top ten list, is a highly effective way of demonstrating your expertise and helping your customers make decisions. The easier you can make the decision process for your customer, the better. The easier the decision, the more likely they will actually buy it! Curation has the added value of being easily shareable on your website and in social media.

TOM'S RECORD LABEL

Tom tours a lot and frequently polls his fans for places to visit or restaurants to eat at, in a variety of locales. This is a form of reverse-curation that heavily involves his fan base. His fans will post their top five places to eat in their hometown. Often times others will comment and add their own lists.

Tom has built his business through a close connection with his fans. He's constantly involved with them on social sites and often curates his top iTunes picks for the month or the top song ideas he's thinking about writing next. For Tom, curation has become an ongoing way to inform and communicate with his fans.

JANE'S PET SHOP

Jane uses curation as a way to add content to her email newsletters, website and blog. Her lists can be interesting as well as educational and useful.

Examples of the lists she's curated:

1. Top ten dogs to own in a big city.

2. Top ten leashes for big dogs.

3. Top ten smartest dogs.

4. Top ten reasons to socialize your dog.

5. Top ten mistakes new dog owners make.

6. Top ten ways to "treat" your dog.

7. Top ten ways to foster a happy pooch.

8. Top ten products all dog owners must have.

9. Top ten new products on the market.

10. Top ten breeds to go running with.

CHAPTER 09
REFERENCES & REFERRALS

Elyse is a personal trainer and most of her business comes from private training sessions. The majority of her new clients come from referrals from current clients. Elyse does two specific things to make sure that her clients continue to refer her to their friends.

First, she's amazing at her job. She makes sure to know what her customers need and want and provides them with the best service possible. In the world of personal training, this includes being on-time, flexible with location and timing to suit her clients' needs, tracking their progress, and knowing how to structure a workout around her clients' specific goals. Elyse makes sure she provides each client with a personalized program that fits his or her goals and needs.

Second, Elyse hosts a free group workout class once a month for all her clients, and they are encouraged to bring their friends. After the class, Elyse offers snacks and drinks as a way of making it comfortable for people to talk and ask questions. She's informative and answers everyone's questions. She makes herself open and doesn't try to force anyone to sign up for training sessions. But from these free classes Elyse inevitably gets new clients. Even if no one signs up that day, they remember her and when the time comes that they decide to invest in a personal trainer, they will most likely call her.

- Do not make your customers work to refer you to their friends.

- Instead, make your customers want to tell others about you.

- How do you make customers want to tell others about you?

- Make it worth their while.

- Be awesome.

DON'T MAKE YOUR CUSTOMERS WORK FOR YOU

What stands out about Elyse is that she doesn't ask her clients to do any work. She offers them something that adds value to being one of her clients. She offers a free class and encourages people to bring friends. She doesn't make it mandatory. She creates a situation where her clients can give something fun to their friends. People are more than happy to invite a friend to a fun, free event. They're passing along something of value to their friend: a free workout.

Do not ask your clients to "work" for you. It will almost never be successful. Let's say you have a vocal coach you practice with once a week. Imagine the coach said to you that she would give you one free session for every 2 people you refer to her. She is basically asking you to do the work of getting her two new clients and she will reward you by giving you one free session. If a single session is $80 is it worth it to you? How many people will you have to approach or call? How much energy and time would it take? Is it really worth it? The answer is probably not.

MAKE REFERRALS AUTOMATIC

Let's say a cheese shop caters many small events such as office, holiday and birthday parties. When the shop puts together the cheese plates for the event they also include cutlery, plates and napkins. On each of these items is the logo for the cheese shop with its address, website and number. The customers like that everything is taken care of for them. They don't have to buy anything else in order to serve the cheese. And everyone at the event knows where the cheese is from. If they like what they are eating they know exactly where to get it. By including the extra items beyond the cheese, the cheese shop adds value to the customer's purchase. And the customer easily refers the cheese shop to her friends without doing any extra work.

MAKE REFERRALS EASY

Sometime a business will give an incentive for referrals. As mentioned earlier, this can be more work for the customer than it's worth. However, this doesn't mean this referral method is completely out of the question. There are ways to do this without forcing work onto your customers.

Let's say a dog walker knows that there are many new puppies in one of the buildings where he has several customers already. Knowing this, his job is to make it easy for his customers to pass on his information. The dog walker might make up cards to give to their customers with contact information, rates and an initial free walk. When someone calls the dog walker and mentions the card, they get a free first walk and the person who gave them the card gets a private, extra-long dog walk. In this situation the dog walker has made it easy for people to refer to him by giving a preprinted card with all the information in one place. They have also made the referral valuable to both parties. And if the dog walker's customers are happy with their dog walker, they will be happy to pass on his information to their neighbors. People like to help others. And they're not only helping, they're giving them the information with a free first walk so there's no pressure. They can try out the dog walker and then make a decision for themselves.

BUY ONE GET ONE FREE

This is a good model for getting your product into the hands of the customers you don't have (yet). This works best for situations where a person can only use one of the product so the extra goes to a friend. Examples of this could be a "buy one get one free" sale on tickets to see a play. You get your ticket and the additional ticket goes to a friend who might not otherwise have come to see the play.

Another example would be for same day hairstyling or haircuts. You get yours and then treat a friend for fre. The idea is to get your customers to refer their friends to you because it adds value to their friend's life. The "BOGO" model works well for situations where your customers want to bring a friend but don't want to convince the friend to spend money on your product. Plays and concerts are good examples of where this method would work well.

REWARD REFERRERS

You have a great service or product and thus your customers refer you to their friends without you doing anything to promote this. This is the best-case scenario. When this happens, the best thing to do is to acknowledge this act and if possible, reward it. If nothing more, say thank you. Say thank you the next time you see them or send them a thank you card. And if it makes sense to go a step further, then do. Steve is a chiropractor and always has his new clients fill out paperwork before their first session. One of the questions asked is how the person chose Steve. When Steve sees that one of his existing patents referred the new client he sends the referring patient a thank you card along with a bottle of wine. How delighted is that referrer! It's such a nice surprise and rest-assured, the old client won't think twice about referring more friends when possible.

BOTTOM LINE

Don't make your clients work to refer you to their friends. Instead, make it fun, make it easy and make them want to do it.

MAKING IT WORK FOR YOU

What is something you can do next week that would inspire your current customers to tell their friends about your business?

1. _____

2. _____

3. _____

TOM'S RECORD LABEL

The best introduction to Tom is to come to a concert. That's why one of the first promotions he ran was "Buy 1 Ticket, Bring a Friend for Free." He figured most people like coming to a concert with a friend but Tom wasn't that popular at the time. So he wanted to encourage fans to bring their friends to a concert without having to make any sort of commitment. So if you came to a show with a valid ticket, you could bring a guest with you.

YouTube serves as another valuable reference model. Most, if not all, of Tom's music is available for free on YouTube. If you like a song, you can easily share it in all the ways that YouTube is shareable, perhaps most importantly on Facebook. Fans also make custom videos with Tom's music.

Digital Marketing for Everyone: Connect with your customers, grow your business

Good

Walden Aisle F   Bay 01 Item 7494

May have some shelf-wear due to normal use.

Prescanned

0KVOFY003S4K

481253476

7814812534 75

19/2021 10:03:31 AM

JANE'S PET SHOP

Jane knows that the best way to get new customers is to approach new dog owners. For this reason she automatically gives a 10% discount to all the dog walkers and dog trainers in the area. She also gives them her "Congratulations on Your New Dog" cards with a 25% off your first purchase discount printed on the back. The trainers and walkers are happy to pass along this savings card to their new clients as a way of giving them something of added value for hiring the dog walker.

Jane's store is beautiful. She knows that people like coming there and once they do, they tend to come back to see the Pooch Picture Wall of Fame, ask her questions and look at the fun dog things she sells. Once a month she sets up a free event for her customers. She calls it a Doggie Mixer. It starts in her shop and a "dog expert" she hires for the hour leads the group. The expert will take the group and teach them something during the hour and then all the dogs and owners walk around the corner to the community dog park. Customers are encouraged to invite other dog owners to the event.

In all Jane's emails she includes a Forward to a Friend link under a special sale post.

CHAPTER 10
SEARCH ENGINE MARKETING

Leia runs a wellness spa in downtown Brooklyn. She is focusing on a very niche market—people in the nearby area who want a massage as part of a bigger focus on their health (not just to relieve sore muscles). She just opened for business and has had a few walk-ins and a few referrals from friends and family.

Leia decides to run an online ad campaign that is as tightly focused as her niche. She wants to run this ad: "Local Brooklyn Wellness Spa, Learn about our Health-Oriented Massage Services, Free 10min Backrubs this Saturday from 12-4" in a few different places. On Google Search, she runs the ad against the keywords "massage" and "healthy living" in her geographic area. On Google Display she chooses websites that talk about living healthy and shows her ad to website visitors who live in her geographic area and are between the ages of 30 and 50. On Facebook she targets her target demographic—women, aged 30-50, income above $65,000, interested in health and fitness, and live within 5 miles of her store.

Within hours of turning on the advertising, traffic to her website has increased markedly. She is directing people to a specific page that shows the spa on a map of the area and describes the Saturday event.

TAKEAWAYS

- Focus your marketing dollars on relevant, targeted traffic.
- Make a succinct, descriptive, specific offer.
- Take the ad viewer to a highly specific landing page.

VERY HIGH RELEVANCE

Think about the last time you were interested in buying something: maybe it was a trip to Italy, a new sofa for your living room, or a used car. There is a good chance you used a search engine, most likely Google, to help you find what you were looking for.

The goal of search engine marketing is to bring together an interested customer and the relevant business. Note the word "relevant." If you are the customer and you are searching for a pair of purple hiking shoes with good ankle support you don't want to be shown blue running shoes. You want a specific item and if by chance this item exists in the world, you want to find it when you enter your search. If you are simply looking for a basic pair of white walking shoes you will of course have more items show up if you enter this information into a Google search, but again, you only want results for white walking shoes.

You use Google to search by typing in a keyword on Google. com (or in a toolbar on your browser) and Google returns a list of websites that are related to what you are looking for. This page is called the search engine results page. And this page is a powerful place for advertisers because you have told Google and the advertisers exactly what you are interested in at this very moment.

The short ads that appear on the side of a Google search results page are the best example of search engine marketing - SEM. We also include Google Display ads and Facebook ads in SEM, because you will use the same thought process to design and run these ads. Display ads are shown on websites next to content rather than on a search engine results page. Ads are shown to users based on the content of the page to make the ads relevant. Facebook ads use demographic targeting to show relevant ads to Facebook users.

GOOGLE ADVERTISING

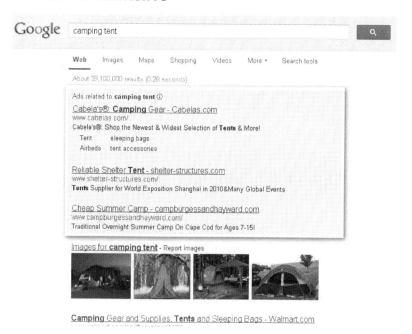

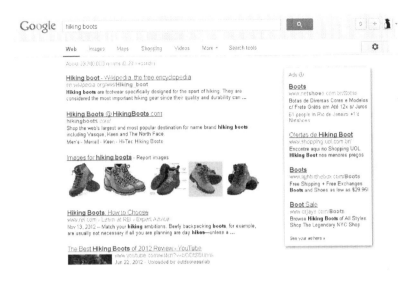

FACEBOOK ADVERTISING

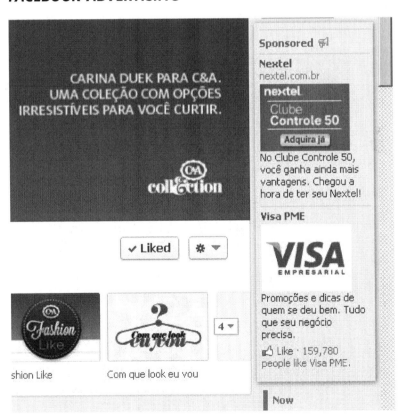

Organic traffic to your website from Google searches seems like it is free, but in reality it takes a great deal of time and energy to develop the content that goes on the website.vcAdditionally, while paid searches cost money for every click you get, so long as the click leads to a sale, the value to a business is positive. SEM is very flexible and can really help attract attention to a specific event or product for a business.

SEM is a huge field with lots of money and users in it (just think Google! This is where a large percentage of their profits come from). The point of this chapter is to give you a short overview of how you can simply leverage this tool for your business. If you want to learn more, we highly recommend the books Advanced Google Adwords by Brad Geddess and Killer Facebook Ads by Marty Weintraub.

USING DIGITAL ADVERTISING

The goal of digital advertising is to deliver targeted, relevant ads to a particular searcher and demographic in order to bring the searcher to your website or landing page so you can make them an offer. The three main components of SEM are:

1. Targeting your demographic – this means choosing the keywords that your target customer types into a search engine, the websites that display the content your target customer is most interested in, and for Facebook, simply describing your demographic.

2. Relevant ads – Ads must attract the attention of your target customer while competing against a lot of other interesting content on the page. To do so, the ads must be highly relevant, targeted, and normally make a very specific offer.

3. Website or landing page—After your potential customer clicks on an ad, they will be directed to a website page of your choice. This page should contain a carefully crafted message that is highly related to the offer you made in your ad. Generally, this means not your website's home page.

KEYWORDS AND DEMOGRAPHIC TARGETING

Google's keyword tool is the best place to start figuring out which keywords people are using on Google to find your product or service. (http://adwords.google.com/o/KeywordTool). The goal of the keyword tool is to develop a list of keywords that you can run advertisements against, both on the search and display network.

You can use your knowledge of your customer demographic as the basis for building your Facebook ads. The Facebook ads tool can be found here: http://www.facebook.com/ads/manage/adscreator.

One of the most interesting components of the Facebook ads tool is the estimate Facebook gives you of how many people you are targeting. It starts with a very big number (the number of Facebook users!) and as you apply filters (such as geography, gender, and other interests) the number starts going down.

WRITING AD COPY

Ads are short. Aim for 25 characters for a header and 70-100 characters for the body. Each place you can put your ads has slightly different requirements. The key for writing good ads is to be as descriptive as possible, given the space constraints. Consider the different products and services you are selling and focus in on a few good reasons people should consider buying from you.

After you come up with a few different versions of your ad, the next step is to test them out. When you have ads live on Google or Facebook, you will generate two important statistics: impressions and clicks. Impressions mean how many times your ad is shown on the Google search engine results page or on the side of a user's Facebook page. Clicks mean how many times a user clicks on one of your ads. You can compare how two different ads are doing by looking at their "click-through rate" or how often an ad is clicked (technically, clicks divided by impressions equal click-through rate). A higher click-through rate is generally better and means your ad is more appealing to your target customer.

The process of looking at click-through rates is called optimization. To optimize your search engine marketing, you will want to remove ads that are not performing well (compared to your other ads) and replace them with new ads. You will then check the new ads to see how they are performing and repeat the process as needed.

LANDING PAGES

Your landing page is the first thing an internet visitor sees after they click on your ad. The most important thing to know about landing pages is they must meet the visitor's expectations as set by the ad. For Leia, she ran the ad "Local Brooklyn Wellness Spa, Learn about our Health-Oriented Massage Services; Free 10min Backrubs this Saturday from 12-4." If the first thing a visitor saw after clicking this ad was the generic homepage for the spa, they would probably be confused. Even worse would be a listing of the spa's services and prices.

Remember, the only thing the visitor knows about Leia's spa is that it is located in Brooklyn, offers massages, and there is a free event on Saturday. The visitor is most likely interested in learning more about the event and probably where it is located! The landing page Leia creates for people who visit her website from the ad should be carefully tailored to give the visitor information related to the offer Leia made in her ad.

MAKING IT WORK FOR YOU

List five keywords and three websites you would buy traffic from. Also write a sample ad for an offer you might have next week.

Keywords:

1. _____

2. _____

3. _____

Websites:

1. _____

2. _____

3. _____

Sample Ad Copy:

Header: _____

Body: _____

BOTTOM LINE

Search engine marketing is a powerful way to tap into the internet to find potential customers. You can target people by their interests as indicated by keywords they type into search engines, the content on the webpages they are reading, or simply their demographics. By writing highly targeted and relevant ads you can attract people's attention, make them an offer, have them click your ad, and take them to a highly targeted and relevant landing page. From there you are well on your way to generating a paying customer!

TOM'S RECORD LABEL

Tom could make use of search engine marketing by thinking about which keywords are closest to his "niche" that his target demographic would use. "Gay musician concert" might be a good possibility. Rather than buying search traffic straight from Google, he would be best served by using display advertising, either on Facebook or Google. If he tried using Facebook, he would use demographic targeting (male, 30-50, gay) to target his ideal customer. He could then run ads about his music or upcoming concerts. He could run similar ads on websites that target gay readers who are interested in music and concerts, using Google's display advertising.

JANE'S PET SHOP

Jane knows that a few of the products she sells are highly popular items. She advertises on keywords that are relevant to someone looking for a specific item in her specific area. For example, in the fall when pets shed, she adds a few Google keyword ads to her advertising budget like "Ferminator" and "Ferminator in Brooklyn". Then when someone in her area was looking for this item the following ad showed: "Ferminators 20% off Sale". She did this for her top ten selling items and made sure that when someone in her neighborhood was looking for an item she carried in her store, it showed up and led them to a page on her website where they could see the item, get it on sale and purchase it.

CHAPTER 11
SEARCH ENGINE OPTIMIZATION

FuguFurniture.com is a company that makes premium inflatable furniture. When the site was first launched most of its traffic was direct, meaning visitors typed FuguFurniture.com directly into the web browser. Thomas, the founder of Fugu, wanted to rank highly in search engines for terms like "inflatable furniture."

We've been talking about how to develop content throughout this book. Visitors to your site come from three main places: direct traffic, referrals from other places like blogs and newspapers, and from search engines like Google. Fugu needed to develop all three of these types of traffic to be successful.

Search traffic, not surprisingly, was very small when Fugu was first launched. Now it gets around 600 unique visitors a month from Google and Bing. The growth in this traffic came from the content on Fugu's page that Google was indexing and from the links Fugu attracted to that content from other reputable and relevant sites. For example, searching for the keyword "inflatable furniture" on Google.fr will bring up Fugu on the first page of results.

TAKEAWAYS

- SEO : Content and links

- Content – All of the text on your website

- Links – Links from other websites back to your website

SEARCH ENGINE OPTIMIZATION

Search engine optimization (SEO) is the technique of making your website appear high in Google (or Bing, to a lesser extent) search results in order to attract visitors to your webpage. SEO boils down to two things: onpage content and links. Having an effective web presence requires having excellent, fresh content, and having excellent, fresh content will naturally lead to other sites linking to yours. If you focus your energies on the part of SEO you can control (content), links and good search engine results will follow.

Every time you type a query into Google, you get back a list of results called a Search Engine Results Page. These results are ordered based on Google's secret algorithm called PageRank. PageRank is Google's best guess about how relevant each page is to the searcher. High relevance will equate to high page rank, which means the page will be shown high on the results page. Appearing high on the results page for a particular search term leads directly to web traffic for the highly placed website. Let's say the keyword "cheap airfare" gets typed into a Google search box 1000 times a day. Of those thousand searches, the vast majority will click on the top three links that appear on the results page. The rest of the searchers will get scattered around on the first page between the lower ranked web pages and on to Google search ads located on the side of the page (and on top of the organic results in a light yellow box). It is not surprising so many businesses are so highly focused on appearing high in the rankings in order to attract searchers to their site!

ONPAGE CONTENT AND BACKLINKS

Google scans the content of just about every page on the web to figure out what the page is about. This is the onpage content. There are all sorts of content you can put on your site: text, pictures, video, audio, and links to other peoples' content. Google is very good at figuring out what your site is about based on onpage content.

Some companies unnecessarily waste their energy into trying to trick Google into ranking them highly. I don't recommend this for anyone, especially not for new and growing companies. Instead, focus your energy on creating the best possible content you can; the more interesting and informative, the better. If you create awesome content, people will talk about it, learn from it, and want to share it with their friends. Every time your site is linked to by another site (perhaps a blogger talking about your product or service), a backlink is created that Google tracks.

Think of links as an ecosystem—people with similar interests will create links back and forth between their sites. You can readily imagine a bookshop having links to author pages but it probably wouldn't have a link to the karate school in the next state. Google looks at all the links going to and from a page in the aggregate and figures out what community the site is part of and how respected the site is in that particular community (also called a niche). The more high quality links from high quality sites one site has, the higher the site's page rank will be.

For any particular small business there aren't any good ways of effectively and time-efficiently gaming Google's system, we strongly caution you against wasting your time trying to do so. Focus on creating high quality content that your interested customers will consume, share, and link to, and the SEO will take care of itself.

NOTE: A general book on marketing can't go into great detail about SEO, nor do we think it is necessary. But given the generally high level of interest in SEO, we recommend picking up the latest iteration of the book SEO for 2012 by Sean Odom and Lynell Allison. In there you can dive as deeply into SEO as you have the desire or time for it.

MAKING IT WORK FOR YOU

Revisit site content you created in the chapter on Website Content – What would be easily shareable?

1. _____

2. _____

3. _____

BOTTOM LINE

SEO gets a lot of attention, mainly because it can drive high quality, relevant traffic to your website. Because of that attention, many entrepreneurs try to figure out how to get their page highly ranked so they can get these coveted search engine visitors. However, in the case of a small business, SEO is rarely worth the time, energy, and resources often devoted to it. The keys to SEO are great content and links, not the dark arts often promoted by shadowy companies on the web. The part of SEO you can most readily control—content—is what you should be spending your marketing efforts improving. Our advice is to focus on the content and let SEO take care of itself.

TOM'S RECORD LABEL

Tom creates a lot of content for other marketing purposes that have powerful SEO effects. All of the videos
that he posts on his site, the tour dates, links back and
forth to interviews, TV shows, and newspaper articles,
music that people share: all this works to generate
good SEO value for his site.

JANE'S PET SHOP

Jane's old website listed only her store hours and location. Thus, even when someone was searching for a pet store in her area, her website didn't show up at the top of the results page. She decided to invest some time and energy into a new site. The new site offers product information including pictures and video demonstrations; it curates products for her neighborhood clientele and much more content, including information on events in her store, photos of the store and clients' pets. Now many pet bloggers link to her site when offering information to their readers; Pinterest pages link to her cute pet photos and her customers share her videos on dog training tips. This is the best thing Jane can do for her site rankings and it has paid off. She might not beat out Petco, but when someone is searching for a pet store or one of her specialty items, it's much more likely that her site will be listed higher than it was a short year ago.

CHAPTER 12
PRIZES

The most famous contest that launched a whole genre of contests is a simple story of "The Oldest Boiler."

A plumber specialized in repairing and replacing very old boilers. His problem was that he didn't know who in his geographic area had a very old boiler. What he needed was a way to get all of his potential customers to identify themselves. He decided to run a contest called "The Oldest Boiler." He advertised that if you sent him a picture of your boiler, whichever boiler was the oldest of all the boilers sent in would be replaced for free.

The promotion was fantastically successful. Replacing a boiler is an expensive and annoying task that most people don't willingly embark on. Running this promotion got the plumber's target audience (people with old boilers that were inefficient and needed to be replaced) to stand up and identify themselves. For the price of replacing one boiler, the plumber now had a prospective customer list. He could target these folks with any type of relevant marketing to help educate them about the value of replacing their boiler.

- Prizes should be of tremendous value to your potential customers.

- Information obtained in exchange for a prize should be of value to your business.

- The prize should make your potential customers identify themselves.

TREMENDOUS VALUE

Prizes and games should always give away something of real value to your customers. The first step in running a promotion or game with a prize is to find out what would be of real value to your potential customers. Odds are that giving away a t-shirt on Facebook won't energize your customer base very much—a t-shirt doesn't have much value. But give away something that people really want and value and they are much more likely to register for your contest.

The options are almost limitless—if you run a coffee shop, let people enter to win free coffee for a month or even a year. If you're a painter, offer to create a free portrait. If you are in a service business, for example web design, figure out what your potential customer's biggest pain point is and offer to solve it for free if they take a 5-minute survey about their needs. Mark and Eleanor, the inn owners from Maine, could give away a free week at the inn for a couple most in need of a vacation.

Once you decide what the prize with tremendous value is, you need to publicize the prize. It should be exciting enough that your target audience will share it naturally with their friends who are also interested in the same thing. For example, if you're an architect who specializes in home renovations, offer to draw up designs to repair the worst-condition home. Solicit photo submissions from homeowners and their friends and family. That way it can become a game for everyone to submit a photo of a house to get a chance to win the prize.

You then need to set up a way that people can enter your contest, typically by giving you their contact information. The easiest way to do that is to have a website page with the contest information and a place for people to submit their email address to enter. You can certainly ask for more information, just know that the more information you ask for, the less likely people are to enter the contest. Plus, you can always start with an email at the beginning, and then request more information as the contest progresses. Whenever you ask for an email address you should ask for permission to contact the owner of the email address. If they don't opt-in for further email contact, make sure to restrict your emails to that person to just contest-related ones.

At the end, you get to choose a winner and give away the prize! You'll want to publicize the winner using your email list and social media and follow up to the non-winners about how your company can provide the service or product they were originally interested in (but did not win). This would be a great time to make an irresistible offer. The architect can offer free in-house consultations. The innkeepers could offer dinner at a local restaurant for every three-night purchase.

MAKING IT WORK FOR YOU

Come up with your own "old boiler" contest.

_____

_____

_____

_____

_____

_____

_____

_____

BOTTOM LINE

Giving away a tremendous prize targeted at just the type of person who would buy from your company is a great way to generate interest in your business and identify your potential customers. The key, like in the oldest boiler, is to make your prize both exciting and compelling enough that your target audience signs up to try and win it. At the end of the contest, you want to have a list of people who are very likely to need and want to buy your product or service.

TOM'S RECORD LABEL

Tom can ask his customers to submit their engagement stories (love is a topic of interest for his demographic) and whoever has the best story can win Tom playing their favorite song at their wedding.

JANE'S PET SHOP

Jane knows that every year a new set of people in her area become pet owners. These are all new customers and she needs a way to find out who they are. She decided to create a contest to identify these people. In her store, on her site, on Facebook and everywhere she could, she posted the contest. It was a "Cutest Puppy" contest and the winner won FREE puppy food for a year. Jane got over a hundred new email addresses of people who were new pet owners, created fun content for her online sites (all the cute photos) and everyone was happy, including the new pet owner who got puppy food for a year.

CHAPTER 13
PREFERRED CUSTOMERS

Shani joins her parents each Sunday night for the family's weekly dinner. They work all week long, but then enjoy their weekend and most of all enjoy the big full dinner they have together on Sunday nights. Although she loves seeing her parents and enjoys the Italian spot they frequent, she never really understands why they insist on going to the exact same restaurant year after year. They even sit in the same booth up near the front.

One week she asked her father if they could try out a new place for her birthday. They ended up at a popular place across town. It's crowded and even though they have a reservation, they have to wait at the bar for 45 minutes before they get a small table in the back. Even after mentioning to the hostess that it's Shani's birthday, they still can't get a better table.

The following week they're back at their regular spot. It's crowded on a Sunday night, but as usual, the family is greeted by name and taken to the perfect table that is ready and waiting for them. Shani's dad remarks that there's just nothing *new* that can ever beat being treated *well*.

TAKEAWAYS

- Make your best customers feel special.

- Give your best customers what they want most.

- Ask your customers what they want - they will tell you!

FREQUENT FLIER MILES : HAPPY CUSTOMERS

Frequent flier programs are one of the best examples of how preferred customers programs work. With all other things equal, a person chooses which airline to fly based on the price of the ticket. Frequent flier programs add value so that the customer has a better experience by flying with one airline over any other. They do this by adding something extra beyond the price of the ticket. One example of added value is getting preferred seating on the flight, sometimes even if you're buying your ticket on an almost sold out flight. Another example is allowing their frequent fliers to cut the line at security checks and board the flight early.

It makes sense. The more someone flies the less hassle they want to encounter and the less time they want to spend with all the waiting that goes into airplane travel. There is an added bonus that comes along with this as well. The added bonus is that these people not only have some hassle taken out of their day, but they also start to feel special. And that's the real kick. People love getting a status upgrade. They like telling their friends that they are a gold or platinum customer. And they love going to the front of the line while everyone else queues up.

MAKE SURE THAT YOUR BEST CUSTOMERS KNOW THAT THEY ARE YOUR BEST CUSTOMERS

Preferred customers are any customers who get something before or above the general public. They're often referred to as loyalty programs, brand ambassadors, or VIP fans.

If you look at your accounts, you'll probably find that your top 20 customers bring in more revenue than your next 20 customers. You'd be foolish not to take note and find ways of making sure you keep those customers. You want to sell more to the customers you already have and use the people most excited about you to drive demand and excitement. Your best customers are also your best representatives outside of your marketing and advertising plans (commonly referred to as word-of-mouth marketing). In some cases, they are your marketing and advertising plans!

INSIDER SALES

Paul Smith, a British clothing store, makes sure to notice when its customers are repeat shoppers and they're good about encouraging these people to continue with that trend. Often the best customers will be invited to the store for a special, private sale. Not only will they get to see a new line of clothing before anyone else, they will get to shop with a special discount usually above 25% off. That's a great deal. And it's great marketing. You know a person is already inclined to purchase your product. You invite them in, give them special attention, a huge discount, and access to items before the general public. They become more than customers, they become friends of the store and brand. And these customers love the special treatment. Of course they'll keep shopping there. Who wants to lose out on this five-star action?

GIVE THEM WHAT THEY WANT, AND MORE OF IT

In order to create your own preferred customer program, where you can reward your own most loyal customers, you must first ask what your customers want. And because they are your best customers, odds are they will tell you! The list will almost undoubtedly include things you never would have considered. It could mean early access to products or services, having their voice heard in the product development cycle, special access to events, preferred pricing, loyalty points, free stuff after a certain number of purchases, and even something as simple as recognition for their contributions to your business.

IDENTIFYING YOUR BEST CUSTOMERS

The easiest way to start a preferred customer program is to invite all of your customers to join. The folks who pay the most attention, the ones who ask you to send them information, are generally your best customers. If you are a coffee shop, leave out "Buy 9, Get the 10th Free" cards by your register ("and only 8 if you're on our email list!") If you're a designer, make sure people know about your Facebook page where you post new work. If you're a band, fans should be on your mailing list so they know when your concerts are.

In some cases it will be obvious who your best customers are. But are they the people who spend a little each day, spend a large amount of money once a year or are very active on your Facebook page? You might want to create programs for more than one type of preferred customer. In some cases, companies identify customers or fans that are very active posting and commenting on their Facebook page. There are customers or fans of your product or work that might be given the right to become a "brand manager" for the day and decide what gets posted or discussed on Facebook. It might be what they really want to do; after all, they're on Facebook all the time anyhow. Some people want the ability to do things other are not allowed to do, some people want gifts, some people want privileges. Get creative, make it something worth your customers' time and energy and make it special.

Once you know what your best customers want, the next step is to put in a plan to deliver.

REAL WORLD APPLICATION

The business world is full of examples. At IBM, the preferred customer program is called "IBM Champions." IBM Champions have to be nominated by a peer. Champions are proponents of IBM that don't work for IBM. They tend to be the highly regarded experts who help implement IBM solutions inside a business. Being nominated is considered quite an honor and being chosen is limited to a select few.

Let's look at why each side would want a Champion program. For IBM, the benefits are from identifying and mobilizing their most ardent supporters. Having independent experts out in the world advocating for IBM software, hardware and services helps IBM sell more of all of these things. As a business, that's the bottom line!

For the Champions, there are equally clear benefits. They get early access to IBM products so they can contribute ideas to their development. This means the end product is better than it would have been and the Champions feel like they are part of the development process and this gives them ownership over the product. IBM officially recognizes Champions as being experts in their field and this helps them win more work or more speaking opportunities. Champions are also invited to mingle together once or twice a year. Putting all those smart people in the same room for a few hours, to recognize the most outstanding Champions, inevitably leads to new connections and new opportunities.

BOTTOM LINE

Creating a "Preferred Customer" program means finding ways to reward your most loyal customers. Ask your most frequent customers how you can make their experience with your business even better! Try including them in insider sales or the product development cycle, or recognizing them for their contributions to your business.

MAKING IT WORK FOR YOU

What extra value can you provide to your best customers?

1. _____

2. _____

3. _____

How are you going to identify your best customers?

1. _____

2. _____

3. _____

TOM'S RECORD LABEL

Everyone on Tom's mailing list is a preferred customer. Recently, Tom released a new album. If you purchased the album during its pre-release dates, you got immediate access to download the music and then would get the physical copy of the CD when it came out. People who weren't on Tom's mailing list would have to wait until the CD was officially released to listen to it. This adds extra value for Tom's preferred customers, because they get to hear the new music long before anyone else. Also, in this latest release, Tom talked a lot about the creative process. Preferred customers got to hear about Tom's artistic process in a way that non-preferred customers did not.

JANE'S PET SHOP

Jane noticed that she had about ten customers who were spending over $300 in her store every month. These were most often her customers with multiple animals and large animals that required a lot of food and accessories each month. She wanted to find a way to make sure they kept coming back to her store.

Today, people can easily order online and have their purchases delivered, so it doesn't always make sense to purchase such a large amount of products in a store and then have to schlep it home. But some people still did this and she wanted to keep them as customers. Jane asked a few of these people the question, "If I could do one thing to help you out what would it be?" One guy laughed and said, "Carry this out to my car!" But most everyone said something about the time they spend getting what they need and getting it home. So Jane decided she would design the Prefurred Pets Program. Now, anyone who spends above a certain amount either within the year or on a consistent basis can call in their order and have it waiting outside and loaded into their car. Also, if someone is within a certain distance, Jane will deliver their orders once a month on a regular basis. They don't even have to come into the store.

Then Jane went one step further. She knew that pet owners love their pets and that her customers might love getting fun freebies from time to time. So along with the delivery and curbside service, she would offer her best customers free samples of new treats that just hit the market, coupons for 25% all toys in the store during the summer, and other neat treats that add value and fun to being a customer at Jane's store.

CHAPTER 14
CONCLUSION

Shani joins her parents each Sunday night for the family's weekly dinner. They work all week long, but then enjoy their weekend and most of all enjoy the big full dinner they have together on Sunday nights. Although she loves seeing her parents and enjoys the Italian spot they frequent, she never really understands why they insist on going to the exact same restaurant year after year. They even sit in the same booth up near the front.

One week she asked her father if they could try out a new place for her birthday. They ended up at a popular place across town. It's crowded and even though they have a reservation, they have to wait at the bar for 45 minutes before they get a small table in the back. Even after mentioning to the hostess that it's Shani's birthday, they still can't get a better table.

The following week they're back at their regular spot. It's crowded on a Sunday night, but as usual, the family is greeted by name and taken to the perfect table that is ready and waiting for them. Shani's dad remarks that there's just nothing *new* that can ever beat being treated *well*.

You most likely picked up this book because you are a creative entrepreneur and wanted advice on how to market yourself, your business, and your product or service. By the time you finish the book you should have filled out at least a few worksheets with ideas that you can begin implementing over the next few days or weeks. We recommend choosing one idea and getting started!

You've also probably realized that many of the tools we recommend are intimately related. Here is how it works for Tom, the barista-turned-rockstar. He starts by creating a new album (content). He talks about the creative process of writing the music and making the CD jacket on Facebook with his fans (social). He lines up all the venues that he will play in during a tour for his fans (partnerships). He releases tickets to the shows and offers a "Buy One, Bring One" deal (referrals). He advertises his tour dates on Google and Facebook to his core demographic and people searching for live music from gay musicians (demographics and search engine marketing). He sends an email to his mailing list inviting them to buy the CD before it is released to the general public (preferred customers). He goes on tour, meets his fans and writes about his traveling experiences on his blog and for the local newspaper (events, SEO). He offers to play live at the wedding of a couple with the best story about how they met (prizes). And he always writes about all of the above and communicates with his fans on Facebook and through email (email, social).

This system wasn't built in a day. By creating great content and offering a fantastic product or service, you too can discover the ideal digital marketing platform for yourself. And remember that you never have to go it alone. Please join other entrepreneurs like yourself on our Facebook page: Facebook.com/groups/Digital-MarketingForEveryone. We feel very privileged that you have made this book part of the way you do business and we look forward to hearing your story.

MAKING IT WORK FOR YOU

1. Think about the list of ideas you've come up with while reading this book. From that list, what is the easiest thing you could actually do tomorrow? Write it down below and **DO IT TOMORROW!**

_____

_____

_____

_____

_____

_____

_____

_____

_____

_____

_____

_____

2. Create a multi-step plan that leverages many of the tools you learned in this book. Think about the example above of how Tom marketed his album: write out five ways you could market one of your products or services that build off each other.

CHAPTER 15
PEOPLE WE LOVE

We owe a huge thank you to the people who read early versions of our manuscript. Thanks Mom! Also Tom Goss and Gabriel Rhoads. Your feedback and advice were taken to heart and incorporated into the book – we couldn't have done it without you. Beau Finley and Adi Segal, thanks for being the last man and woman reviewing and making sure every last typo and awkward phrase was eliminated.

Also a massive thank you to all of our students and clients. The awesome work you do is what inspires us to teach and to write.

Thank you to all the places that have had us in to teach about digital marketing. Above all thanks to J. Perelmuter and the 3rd Ward for giving us our first shot at teaching 'Digital Marketing for Everyone'.

- The 3rd Ward (NYC)

- Republikken (Copenhagen, Denmark)

- Lynfabrikken (Aarhus, Denmark)

- Copenhagen Business School: School of Entrepreneurship (Copenhagen, Denmark)

- General Assembly (NYC, London, Berlin)

- Betahaus (Berlin)

- Le Camping (Paris, France)

- Catchafire (NYC)

- Association of Collaborative Professionals (NYC)

- Mutinerie (Paris, France)

Thanks to Samira Villamor for conceiving and creating our kickass cover. Can't wait to work with you again for the next one. And to Bruna Barretto for the wonderful layout work on the 2nd edition.

CHAPTER 16
ABOUT US

ERIC MORROW

Eric Morrow is a digital marketer with IBM. He received his BA in Political Economy from the University of California: Berkeley and his JD from the Georgetown University Law Center. He has helped large multi-national companies and individual artists and professionals tap into the power of digital media to win more customers.

SHANNON CHIRONE

Shannon Chirone works in digital marketing in the entertainment industry. She graduated from the University of California, Los Angeles. Since moving to New York she's worked with prominent music artists as well as small business owners on developing and implementing their digital strategy.

Made in the USA
San Bernardino, CA
03 October 2017